EX LIBRIS.   £ 4.99
             ABC12

Reg Swinfton

TOUCH WOOD

A Journey Among Trees

TOUCH WOOD

A Journey Among Trees

**Photographs taken and text chosen by
HERBERT WHONE**

First published in 1990 by
SMITH SETTLE
Ilkley Road, Otley,
West Yorkshire LS21 3JP

ISBN   Paperback 1 870071 50 6
        Hardback   1 870071 51 4

Designed, printed and bound by
SMITH SETTLE
Ilkley Road, Otley
West Yorkshire LS21 3JP

Literary Contents

Where material is not generally known, the author's source is indicated – though this is not necessarily the first edition.

p 70 poem by Emily Dickinson from *Complete Poems of Emily Dickinson* — Little, Brown & Co., Boston 1924

p 72 poem *The Trees of the Garden* (Sonnet LXXXIX) by Dante Gabriel Rossetti

p 73 poem *A Dumb Friend* by Christina Rossetti

p 75 from *The Year* by Lord Dunsany — Jarrolds 1946

p 76 poem *The Oak Tree* by William Barnes, from *Poems of Rural Life in Dorset Dialect* — Kegan Paul 1879

p 79 from the poem *Yardley Oak* by William Cowper

p 81 poem *The Round Oak* by John Clare, from *The Later Poems of John Clare* — Manchester University Press (Robinson & Summerfield ed.) 1964

p 82 extract from the *Egyptian Book of the Dead*

p 82 from *Trees Shown to the Children* by Kelman and Smith — Jack Ltd. 1908

p 82 poem *The Sycamore Tree* by F. E. Stutchbury — pub. in the anthology *Trees* — Society of the Men of the Trees 1947

p 83 from *A House* by Ford Madox Ford, in *The Chapbook for 1921* — The Poetry Bookshop

p 84 poem *The Birch* by Wilfrid Gibson, from *Islands; Poems 1930-32* — Macmillan 1932

p 84 poem *Trees* by W. H. Davies, from *Collected Poems* — Jonathan Cape 1963

p 85 extract from a letter by William Blake written in 1799 to Rev Dr Trusler

p 87 from *The Romance of Names* by Ernest Weekley — Murray 1914

p 88 poem by Glyn Hughes from *Rest the Poor Struggles* — Macmillan 1972

p 88 poem *In a Myrtle Shade* from the Rossetti MS, by William Blake

p 88 poem *A Seed* by William Allingham, from *Poems by William Allingham* — Macmillan 1912

p 91 from *The Sylvan Year* by Philip Gilbert Hammerton — Seeley, Jackson & Halliday 1876

p 91 No. 3 from *Season Songs* by Ted Hughes — Faber & Faber 1976

p 92 poem *Under a Wiltshire Apple Tree* by Anna de Bary, from *New & Selected Lyrics*; quoted in de la Mare's *Come Hither* 1923

p 94 poem *Mutability* by Rainer Maria Rilke, from *The Book of Images,* in *Selected Works of R. M. Rilke* — Hogarth Press 1960

p 96 poem *The Tree* by John Freeman, from *Poems New and Old* — Selwyn & Blount 1920

p 97 poem *Autumn* by Rainer Maria Rilke (as page 94)

p 99 from *The Winged Destiny: Studies in the Spiritual History of the Gael* by Fiona MacLeod (William Sharp) — Heinemann 1910

p 101 from *Watership Down* by Richard Adams — Rex Collins 1972

p 102 from *The Lord of the Rings* by J. R. R. Tolkien — George Allen & Unwin 1954

p 104 poem *The Tree Uprooted* by Dora Sigerson Shorter, from *The Sad Years* — Constable 1918

p 104 from an article in *The Times,* 19 October 1987

p 105 from *Sylva: A Discourse of Forest Trees* by John Evelyn (1706 edition)

p 107 poem *Ten O'clock No More* by John Freeman, from *Georgian Poetry* — the Poetry Bookshop 1920

p 108 poem *Willows* by Reginald Arknell, from *More Green Fingers* — Herbert Jenkins Ltd. 1938

p 108 poem *The Willow* by Walter de la Mare, from *The Veil and Other Poems* — Constable & Co. 1921

p 109 from the poem *Under The Willows* by James Russell Lowell, from *The Poetical Works of Lowell* — Ward Lock & Co.

p 110 poem *Trees* by Alfred Joyce Kilmer, from *Trees and Other Poems* — Dowan, New York 1914

p 110 poem *Silver Birch* by Teresa Hooley, from *Selected Poems* — Jonathan Cape 1947

p 113 poem *The Rowan Tree* by Baroness Nairne (Caroline Oliphant), from *Life and Songs of the Baroness Nairne* — Griffin 1872

p 113 postscript to a sequence of poems *On a Deserted Shore* by Kathleen Raine — Hamish Hamilton 1973

p 114 poem *The Old Tree* by Andrew Young, from *Collected Poems* — Jonathan Cape 1936

p 115 poem *Dead Tree* by Abel Stanion

p 116 and 118 from *Wandering* by Hermann Hesse (trans. James Wright) — Jonathan Cape 1972

p 119 from *Essays* (Nature) by Ralph Waldo Emerson

p 120 from the poem *I Remember, I Remember* by Thomas Hood

p 120 poem *My Cathedral* by Henry Wadsworth Longfellow

p 122 from *Our Village* by Mary Russell Mitford

p 124 excerpts from *Stray Birds* by Rabindranath Tagore — Macmillan 1917

p 125 from *Memories, Dreams, Reflections* by C. G. Jung

p 127 from *English Woodlands and their Story* by Houghton Townley — Methuen & Co. 1910

p 128 from *The Golden Bough* by J. G. Frazer

p 131 from *Gods and Myths of Northern Europe* by H. R. Ellis Davidson — Penguin 1964

p 133 from *Walden*, or *Life in the Woods* by H. D. Thoreau

p 135 from *The Art of Creation* by Edward Carpenter — George Allen & Unwin 1904

p 136 from *Polynesian Mythology* by Sir George Grey — Routledge 1905

p 139 from the Holy Bible: Job 14 v.1–10

p 139 poem *The Aspen* from *Carmina Gadelica* by A. Carmichael — Constable 1900

p 140 from the poem No. LXX from *Underwood* by Ben Jonson

p 140 poem *Outlived by Trees* by Siegfried Sassoon, from *Rhymed Ruminations* — Faber & Faber 1940

p 142 from *Mythology of the Soul* by H. G. Baynes — Balliere, Tindale & Cox 1940

p 145 from *Heaven and Hell* by Emanuel Swedenborg

p 146 epitaph from Low Leyton Church, quoted in *Chronicles of the Tombs* by T. J. Pettigrew — H. G. Bohn 1857

p 186 from *Sylva – A Discourse of Forest Trees* by John Evelyn

p 187 from *Far Away and Long Ago* by W. H. Hudson – Dent (Everyman)

p 188 and 190 from *The Woodlanders* by Thomas Hardy

p 191 poem *The Fallen Elm* by John Clare, from *The Poems of John Clare* – Dent (J. W. Tibble ed.) 1935

p 192 from *The Long Exile and Other Stories for Children* by Leo Tolstoi

p 194 from *The Centuries* by Thomas Traherne

p 195 from *The Music of a Tree* by W. J. Turner, from *The Hunter and Other Poems* – Sidgwick & Jackson 1916

p 196 Chinese poem by Po Chui-I, trans. by Arthur Waley – George Allen & Unwin 1946

p 199 from *The Children's Blue Bird,* an adaptation of Maeterlinck's *The Blue Bird* by Georgette Leblanc-Maeterlinck – Methuen & Co. 1913

p 200 from *Puck of Pook's Hill* by Rudyard Kipling

p 203 poem *The Wood-Maze* by Laurence Housman – W. Heinemann 1919

p 204 poem *What do the Trees Say* by Anne MacDonald, from *Dormer Windows* – Collins 1923

p 204 poem *In Burnham Beeches* by Andrew Young – Martin Secker & Warburg 1936

p 205 from *As You Like It* by W. Shakespeare (Act III Scene 2)

p 207 from *Lost Forest* by Dorothy Wellesley, from *Selected Poems* – Williams & Norgate 1949

p 208 from *A Witch's Guide to Gardening* by Dorothy Jacob – Elek Books 1964

p 210 poem *The Fairy Thorn* by Sir Samuel Ferguson, from *Irish Tales* ed. by W. B. Yeats – Walter Scott Press 1893

p 211 from *Portrait of Elgar* by Michael Kennedy – O.U.P. 1987

p 213 poem *Trees in the Moonlight* by James Reeves, from *The Complete Poems for Children* – Heinemann 1973

p 214 from *Heroes of Asgard* by A. and E. Keary – Macmillan

p 217 poem *The Two Trees* by W. B. Yeats, from *The Collected Poems* – Macmillan 1948

p 218 from *In the Fall* by Hugh MacDiarmid, from *The Hugh MacDiarmid Anthology* – Routledge & Kegan Paul 1972

p 220 from *Marmion* by Sir Walter Scott

p 222 poem *The Hill Pines Were Sighing* by Robert Bridges, from *Shorter Poems* – George Bell & Sons 1896

p 223 poem No. I from a sequence *Cherry Tree Poems* by John Purser – Aquila Pub. Co. 1976

p 224 from *Sylva: A Discourse of Forest Trees* by John Evelyn

p 224 poem *Tree Planting* by Alfred Noyes, from *Shadows on the Down* – Hutchinson & Co. 1945

p 225 report from *The Yorkshire Post,* 13 March 1989

p 226 poem *A Tree in the City* by Caryll Houselander, from *The Flowering Tree* – Sheed & Ward Ltd. 1945

p 227 poem *Child's Song in Spring* by Edith Nesbit, from *A Pomander of Verse* – John Lane 1895

p 228 from *Hampshire Days* by W. H. Hudson – Longmans & Co. 1903 p 230 from the poem *Lines Written in Early Spring* by William Wordsworth

p 231 from *Edge of Darkness, Edge of Light* by R. C. Scriven – Souvenir Press 1977

p 232 and 233 from *The Gospel of the Essenes,* trans. by E. Bordeaux Szekeley – C. W. Daniel Co. Ltd.

p 234 extract from *Pagan and Christian Creeds* by Edward Carpenter – George Allen & Unwin 1920

p 235 extract from an English Emblem book *Ashrea* by E. M. 1665 (exact authorship uncertain)

p 236 poem by Francis Thompson, from *Poems of Francis Thompson* – Burns Oats & Washbourne 1913

p 237 from *The Faerie Queene* by Edmund Spenser

p 238 extract from article by Tessa Robertson in *WWF Journal* 1988

p 238 extract from a pamphlet by the Woodland Trust

Copyright Acknowledgements

Permission to use copyright material is gratefully acknowledged to the following:

Anthony Clarke Publishers for *Seeds of Contemplation* by Thomas Merton

Unwin Hyman Ltd. for extracts from *The Lord of the Rings* by J. R. R. Tolkien; the poem *The Trees* from *Poems* by E. L. Davison; the poem from *Chinese Poems* trans. by Arthur Waley

George T. Sassoon for the poem *Outlived by Trees* from *Rhymed Ruminations* by Siegfried Sassoon

A. P. Watt (Literary Agents) on behalf of Irene Collis, for an excerpt from *The Vision of Glory* by John Stewart Collis; also an excerpt from *The Golden Bough* by J. G. Frazer

Martin Secker & Warburg Ltd. for the poems *The Old Tree* and *In Burnham Beeches* from *Collected Poems* by Andrew Young

Thames & Hudson Ltd. for an excerpt from *Myth and Ritual in Christianity* by Alan W. Watts

Faber & Faber Ltd. for a poem from *Symmetries and Asymmetries* by W. H. Auden; part 3 of *Autumn Nature Notes* from *Season Songs* by Ted Hughes; the poem *The Tree* from *Collected Shorter Poems* by Ezra Pound; an extract from *A Country Child* by Alison Uttley; the poem *The Magic Wood* from *Black Seasons* by Henry Treece

Curtis Brown Group Ltd, on behalf of the Estate of Lord Dunsany, for verses from *The Year* by Lord Dunsany

James MacGibbon, executor of Stevie Smith for the poem *Little Boy Lost* from *The Collected Poems of Stevie Smith* (Penguin Modern Classics)

Jonathan Cape Ltd. for the poem *Silver Birch* from *Selected Poems* by Teresa Hooley; the poem *Trees* from *The Complete Poems* by W. H. Davies

Jonathan Cape and the Estate of Hermann Hesse, for an extract from *Wandering* by Hermann Hesse (trans. by James Wright)

Hamish Hamilton Ltd. for the poem from *On a Deserted Shore* by Kathleen Raine

Mr Michael Gibson and Macmillan (London and Basingstoke) for the poem *The Birch* from *Islands 1930–32* by Wilfrid Gibson

John Murray Publishers Ltd. for an excerpt from *The Romance of Names* by Ernest Weekley; part of the poem *The Song Tree* from *Collected Poems* by Alfred Noyes; an excerpt from A. J. Arberry's translation of *The Discourses* by Jalal al-Din Rumi

Glyn Hughes for his poem from *Rest the Poor Struggles*

The Estate of Rainer Maria Rilke, St John's College (Oxford) and Chatto & Windus/Hogarth Press, for the two poems *Mutability* and *Autumn* from *Selected Works Vol 2* by R. M. Rilke

Mrs Laura Huxley for the poem *The Elm* from *Collected Poems* by Aldous Huxley

Richard Adams and Penguin Books Ltd. for an excerpt from *Watership Down* by Richard Adams

Century Hutchinson Ltd. for the poem *The Willows* from *More Green Fingers* by Reginald Arkell

The Literary Trustees of Walter de la Mare and The Society of Authors for the poem *The Willow* by Walter de la Mare

Collins Publishers for an excerpt from *The Lion, the Witch, and the Wardrobe* by C. S. Lewis; an excerpt from *Memories, Dreams, Reflections* by C. J. Jung

Penguin Books Ltd. for an excerpt from *Gods and Myths of Northern Europe* by H. R. Ellis Davidson 1964

Balliere, Tindale, Cox, for an excerpt from *Mythology of the Soul* by H. G. Baynes

James Clarke & Co Ltd. (Lutterworth Press) for two excerpts from *I Planted Trees* by Richard St Barbe-Baker

J. M. Dent & Sons Ltd. for an excerpt from *British Trees* by Miles Hadfield; the poem *The Wych-Elm* by Richard Church

Grafton Books (A Division of Collins Publishing Group) for an excerpt from *The Perpetual Forest* by W. B. Collins

Hugh MacDiarmid and Routledge & Kegan Paul for part of the poem *In the Fall* by Hugh MacDiarmid, from *The Hugh MacDiarmid Anthology*

Souvenir Press Ltd. for an excerpt from *Edge of Darkness, Edge of Light* by R. C. Scriven

Norma Bordeaux Szekeley for two excerpts from *The Essene Gospel of Peace* (British Edition entitled *The Gospel of the Essenes*), by E. Bordeaux Szekeley

Sidgwick & Jackson Ltd. for the poem *The Music of a Tree* from *The Hunter and Other Poems* by W. J. Turner

William Heinemann for the poem *The Wood-Maze* from *Heart of Peace* by Laurence Housman

The James Reeves Estate for the poem *Trees in Moonlight* from *The Complete Poems for Children* (Heinemann) James Reeves

Anne Dunford for her poem *Green*

Abel Stanion for his poem *Dead Tree*

John Purser and Aquila Publishing Co. Ltd. for *Cherry Tree Poem* (I) from *The Counting Stick* by John Purser

Mowbray Publishers for an excerpt from *Life of St Bernard* by William of Thierry, trans. by Geoffrey Webb and Adrian Walker (1960)

Oxford University Press for an excerpt from *Portrait of Elgar* by Michael Kennedy (1987 edition)

H. C. E. Noyes for the poem *Tree Planting* from *Shadows on the Down* by Alfred Noyes

The family of Dorothy Wellesley and the Curator of the Duke of Wellington for part of the poem *The Lost Forest* by Dorothy Wellesley

Editions Juillard, Paris for the poem *Tree that I Love* from *First Poems* by Minoue Drouet, trans. by Margaret Crosland

Manchester University Press for the poem *The Round Oak* from *The Later Poems of John Clare* (Robinson & Summerfield ed.)

WWF (World Wide Fund for Nature) and Tessa Robertson for an excerpt from an article by her in *WWF Journal* 1988

The Times Newspapers Ltd for an extract from an article on gales of 1987 by Paul Vallely

The Woodland Trust for an extract from a pamphlet

Yorkshire Post Newspapers Ltd for an article ot 13 March 1989

In one or two instances, it has been impossible to trace authors or copyright ownership. I apologise for any omission and will make amends should these come to light.

Introduction

This book is the culmination of a life-long fascination. I am not alone, I know: many people have loved trees. They are part of the back-cloth of nature against which we live our lives, and which we take so much for granted. Present day materialistic values and self interest have blinded many to nature's beauty and mystery – one of the heavy prices we pay for what we call progress: but despite this, to free themselves from their prison, human beings turn instinctively to nature as a healing balm. And what in nature is more omnipresent than the tree? What would life be without trees? Is there anyone, I wonder, who at one time or another has not pondered on the generations of human life a particularly old tree has witnessed; or who has not looked with childlike wonderment at the delicately veined leaves of the sycamore, or watched the miracle of the opening of the horse-chestnut buds in spring? Who has not walked through a wood at dusk and mistaken some strange shape for a lurking animal and felt a chill in the spine; or who has not seen a tree fighting for its life under the ferocity of a winter gale? But I will not enumerate any further the attributes of the tree – they are expressed in a variety of ways by the authors whose words accompany the images in this book.

The words chosen differ widely as to time and style, but nevertheless have in them a universality of feeling – they contain nothing which at some level I do not recognise in my own experience. Despite our differences we are all human; and a tree is a tree whatever its label may say. The quotations are all facets of a whole, touching in their own way upon the essence of the tree – its *treeness*. Moreover, in them we may detect the common bond and correspondence between human life and tree life the various authors have felt.

Of that correspondence there can be no doubt: the tree has been closely involved in the life of man from the beginning of time. Not only was the tree the ruler of nature, beside which a man felt dwarfed, but deeper than that it was the expression of a primal life-force and pattern, the so-called Tree of Life which is to be found in most religions. Man himself is part of this Tree. It is a Tree whose life and pattern is a unit, and yet which comprises a trinity of functions. The roots dig deep into the dark earth for nourishment; the trunk, with its life-blood the sap, pushes upwards; whilst the leaves, benefiting from the nourishment below, reach out to the light of the sun without which life is impossible. Are not we human beings, though freer to move about, part of this scheme? We are rooted to the earth by the appetites of the physical body; we have a life of the soul tied to the latter but able to reach upwards to spiritual heights; and we have the pure Spirit. The growth that takes place in the soul depends both on material existence and on the Light and Intelligence of the Son, the Divine Mind – just as nature's plant depends on the earth and on the light of the sun for its flowering: a trinity of Body, Soul, Spirit. There

are, of course, other ways of seeing this trinity but always we find polar opposites held in working relationship by a third mediating and more flexible force.

There are many aspects of this correspondence between tree and man. As a lone tree might grow to its perfect form were it not subjected to gales, frost, and the struggle against its fellows for nourishment, so might a human being be able to grow untroubled into maturity were it not for the resistance offered by his fellows and the vagaries of fate. As it is, in the process of growth, there is as much opposition for the tree as for man. Further, if all nature is seen as an evolving struggle towards one objective, the realisation of man's potential as an Image of God, we may see how all her different forms and functions are inter-dependent and inter-penetrating. There is nothing in nature, as with the individual cell in relation to the human body, which is not a necessary part of the whole. It is not surprising therefore, that a tree's characteristics are reflected in other living beings, animal and human – nor that a man, though he sees the tree as being outside him, also feels it as something alive within him. As a microcosm, *all* is within him.

Also, in looking at a tree, men come face to face with the greatest of all life's mysteries, the secret of generation – the process of birth, growth and transformation in and from the microscopic seed to a final structure of immense size. They come face to face with the mystery of the formative Intelligence, the Idea or Image behind and in each formal structure, by which a living being becomes what it is and no other. Is there any wonder, taking these considerations alone, that the tree has always been an object of awe and veneration!

As to the writing of the book itself, it really started in childhood in the woods near my birthplace, Bingley, a West Riding industrial town in a beautiful natural setting. There I absorbed the spirit of the trees against an ever-changing background of weather and seasons. I played amongst them, climbed them, and was taken for walks amongst them on Sundays. At an early age I found myself noticing strange shapes in their trunks – the same ferocious or gentle shapes assumed by the clouds that moved past the window as I lay ill in bed, or that flickered in the flames of the kitchen fire on winter evenings. At fourteen, my father presented me with my first box camera and among the first attempts are trees beautified by snow. Later, at sixteen, my first pencil sketches invariably had trees in the foreground. At school, in wood-work classes I watched the transformation of a crude block of sycamore into the beautiful smooth finish after planing and French polishing, and found it by far the most satisfying activity in the curriculum.

Then followed a period of stunted growth, as far as trees were concerned. As a student in war-scarred Manchester, and then during work in London, professional ambition tended to rule life, though I took to nature whenever the opportunity arose. But the interest was only dormant. In Scotland, the wild aspects of nature and of trees in particular, cast their spell again, and at a time of compulsive oil painting, I joined trees and city (Glasgow) together, in an exhibition in the Douglas Foulis Gallery, Edinburgh. The trees were noticeably gaunt and battling against the elements. This combination of town and tree theme continued in exhibitions in Glasgow in the early 60's, until the fascination of Glasgow itself took over, the textured quality of its buildings worn by the elements seeming little different from that of the trees themselves.

As a professional musician carrying on this double life, I returned to Yorkshire in 1965, and immediately trees began to figure in landscape paintings of the industrial West Riding. The wheel was beginning to turn full circle. In 1973, with a camera to hand during country walks, I began to record trees in all their magnificence and unpredictability, and in the following year did a series of about 70 pen sketches which were more a means of studying their unique personalities than works of art. These drawings were eventually shown along with the tree photographs in the Harrogate Art Gallery, and then lay fallow until this book was conceived later. Trees were never far from my thoughts, however, as two later essentially photographic books, one on the West Riding and the other on Fountains Abbey, testify. It is due to Mr Ken Smith of Smith Settle, publishers and printers responsible for these earlier books, that the body of the work collected over the years came to be presented in its present form.

Clearly the book is not based on botanical or scientific research, and there are innumerable aspects of the tree, mythological, ecological, and other, which are not touched upon. It is purely one man's attempt to convey the essence of the tree world, helped by the words of writers who like myself have been under its spell. To all these artists, dead or living, I am deeply grateful. The matching of words with photographs, for a variety of reasons, has its limits, and though there is a thread holding them together, it is a loose one, and there has been no attempt to make an exact one-to-one correspondence. There is, for example, a disproportionate amount of literature on the oak, and conversely, the elder, which has interesting properties in country lore, is not particularly photogenic. Also for obvious reasons I have had to be selective and omit some poems I admire. As to the photographs themselves, I make no apology for the fact that many are taken in the seasons of spring, autumn and winter, when trees can be *seen*, so to speak. In the summer, the mass of foliage disguises their essential structure and character, in addition to which there is little subtlety in the lighting. And of course, I am not without sadness about the lack of colour, especially with pictures taken in autumn. Something is inevitably lost, but every medium involves sacrifice of some sort, and the two modes of perception are quite different. For the interest of photographers, the photographs were all unstaged and spontaneous gifts to the eye, to be caught immediately or lost. The degree to which this is true may be seen in the fact that on the odd occasion when a picture was unsatisfactory,

and I had to return to the original site in order to retake, the lighting was never exactly right and I ended by using the first attempt.

I do not apologise either for constantly returning to childhood impressions, or for the mystical bias to the book. Life is a mystery. I have learned that I know very little, but like others, still seek to unravel some of that mystery – or rather, pray it will be revealed in time. But I have no doubt that all life, as to its physical manifestation, has a spiritual root – that its forms emanate from a creative source sometimes referred to as the Mind of God, about which, as a result of the prison of the time process and man's limited rational mind, we have little knowledge. As I have said, the acorn which becomes an immense oak tree is a mystery under our very noses. Could we but see, further than our two eyes allow, the process whereby this takes place, we would have broken through the veils hiding Eternity – a privilege which for good reason is temporarily denied most mortals. Tennyson expresses this wonderment in meditating upon a small flower, which could equally be read as a tree. . . .

> Flower in the crannied wall,
> I pluck you out of the crannies,
> I hold you here, root and all, in my hand,
> Little flower – but if I could understand
> What you are, root and all, and all in all,
> I should know what God and man is.

How many human beings, from the beginning of time have, I wonder, shared such a sense of awe before the smallest of flowers and before the mightiest of trees.

With this mystery in mind, I share the concern felt by many about the fate of nature and of the earth itself in this technological age. Nature is undeniably being abused in the interests of scientific advancement and of mammon – and there is no doubt now that trees are increasingly in danger from both ruthless felling and various forms of pollution. I myself have witnessed, in the last few years, the uprooting of several fine trees in the interests of an easier passage for the plough, and of bigger and better fields. What, I wonder, would have been the feelings of the writers quoted in this book at this state of affairs. For them, the health of the tree was something taken for granted. Now it is a question of survival – the most commonplace and yet the greatest wonder of nature must be protected if future generations of child and man are to continue to stand before it in the same awe and spirit of reverence. Societies like the Men of the Trees, the Woodland Trust, the Friends of the Earth, and the World Wide Fund for Nature are doing wonderful work towards ensuring this happens, and deserve continual support in their preservation and re-planting programmes.

Finally, it would be a disservice to the tree were I not to mention that as a professional violinist, I have had (though for long, unwittingly) the most intimate of connections with it in my music making. The 'touch wood' in the title of the book refers of course to the cross of Christ, but in touching the wood of the violin to life through the bow, and eliciting from it the most expressive sound of any musical instrument except for the voice itself, human beings are transported into a world scarcely less magical.

This book, as I said, is the culmination of a life-long fascination. I know well that the viewpoint of one man will have its shortcomings. Nevertheless I have aimed to find the Tree which is beyond personal vision. If I have succeeded in this to some degree, and helped people to look again at what they have begun to take for granted, my work will have been worthwhile.

HERBERT WHONE
HARROGATE 1989

Footnote:

I would like to acknowledge my indebtedness to Philip Tennant of Tennant Brown, photographers of Harrogate, for his part in the book. He produced enlargements from the negatives, generously giving of his time until each picture was as I had conceived it. Without such co-operation and technical skill there would have been no book.

Only in places where I felt it might interest the reader has the specific place or locality where the photographs were taken been indicated in the index.

Dedication

This book is dedicated to all friends of trees young or old

A Fool sees not the same tree that a wise man sees.

WILLIAM BLAKE
from *The Marriage of Heaven and Hell*

A TREE gives glory to God first of all by
being a tree. For in being what God means
it to be, it is imitating an idea which
is in God and which is not distinct from
the essence of God, and therefore a tree
imitates God by being a tree.

The more it is like itself, the more it
is like Him. If it tried to be something
else which it was never intended to be, it
would be less like God and therefore it
would give Him less glory.

But there is something more. No two trees
are alike. And their individuality is no
imperfection. On the contrary: the
perfection of each created thing is not
merely in its conformity to an abstract
type but in its own individual identity
with itself. This particular tree will
give glory to God by spreading out its roots
in the earth and raising its branches into
the air and the light in a way that no other
tree before or after it ever did or will
do.

Do you imagine that all the individual
created things in the world are imperfect
attempts at reproducing an ideal type
which the Creator never quite succeeded
in actualizing on earth? If that is so
they do not give Him glory but proclaim
that He is not a perfect Creator.

Therefore each particular being, in its
individuality, its concrete nature and
entity, with all its own characteristics
and its private qualities and its own
inviolable identity, gives glory to God
by being precisely what He wants it to be
here and now, in the circumstances
ordained for it by His Love and
His infinite Art.

from *The Seeds of Contemplation*
by THOMAS MERTON (1915–1968)

EVEN to this day St. Bernard claims that it was by
praying and meditating in the woods and the fields
that he discovered the deep meaning of Holy Writ.
He jokingly says to his friends that it was only the
oaks and the beeches who were his masters in this subject.

from *The Life of St. Bernard (1091–1153)*
by WILLIAM OF THIERRY (1085–1148)

Man

MAN doth usurp all space,
Stares thee, in rock, bush, river, in the face.
Never yet thine eyes beheld a tree;
'Tis no sea thou seest in the sea,
'Tis but a disguised humanity.
To avoid thy fellow, vain thy plan;
All that interests a man, is man.

HENRY SEPTIMUS SUTTON (1825–1901)

Voice of the Trees

UNTO us is given the Pattern of the Tree,
The Tree of Life Divine—of Immortality;
Thus do we grow—to copy limb for limb
The greatest work of God,—the very Life of Him.
Reaching for the Light, our roots still in the earth,
Heaven would we gather to hold within our girth,
That with the sap commingled when ascent is made
In Springtime, then out-leafed will Heaven be displayed.

CATHERINE BLAKISTON (pub. 1955)

AND just as the roots of the tree
Sink into the earth and are nourished,
And the branches of the tree
Raise their arms to heaven,
So is man like the trunk of the tree,
With his roots deep
In the breast of his Earthiy Mother,
And his soul ascending
To the bright stars of his Heavenly Father.
And the roots of the tree
Are the Angels of the Earthly Mother,
And the branches of the tree
Are the Angels of the Earthly Father.
And this is the sacred Tree of Life
Which stands in the Sea of Eternity.

from *The Gospel of the Essenes*
(circa 100 B.C. – A.D.17) **trans.**

6

OLD Yew, which graspeth at the stones
  That name the under-lying dead,
  Thy fibres net the dreamless head,
Thy roots are wrapt about the bones.

The seasons bring the flower again,
  And bring the firstling to the flock;
  And in the dusk of thee, the clock
Beats out the little lives of men.

O not for thee the glow, the bloom,
  Who changest not in any gale;
  Nor branding summer suns avail
To touch thy thousand years of gloom:

And gazing on thee, sullen tree,
  Sick for thy stubborn hardihood,
  I seem to fail from out my blood
And grow incorporate into thee.

from *In Memoriam* by
ALFRED LORD TENNYSON (1809–1892)

ALL under the leaves, the leaves of life,
I met with virgins seven,
And one of them was Mary mild,
Our Lord's mother from heaven.

'O what are you seeking, you seven fair maids,
All under the leaves of life?
Come tell, come tell me what seek you
All under the leaves of life?'

'We're seeking for no leaves, Thomas,
But for a friend of thine;
We're seeking for sweet Jesus Christ,
To be our guide and thine.'

'Go you down, go you down to yonder town,
And sit in the gallery;
And there you'll find sweet Jesus Christ,
Nailed to a big yew-tree.'

So down they went to yonder town,
As fast as foot could fall,
And many a grievous bitter tear,
From the virgins' eyes did fall.

'O peace, mother, O peace, mother,
Your weeping doth me grieve;
O I must suffer this,' he said,
'For Adam and for Eve.'

from *The Seven Virgins*,
a traditional carol

As is well known, the Cross and the Sacrificial Tree are symbols far more ancient than Christianity, and had a significance of such importance that it is not at all inappropriate for the hymn to say:

> *Sola digna tu fuisti*
> Ferre mundi victimam.

> Thou alone (the Tree) wert found *worthy*
> to bear the Victim of the world.

So many of the hero-gods and *avatars* are associated with the Tree that the central symbol of Christianity is of a truly universal nature, and by no means a historical abnormality. In the myth of Osiris, "he who springs from the returning waters", the body of the God—slain by Set the Evil One—is found within a giant tamarisk or pine-tree which had been cut down and used for the *central pillar* of the Palace of Byblos. Attis, son of the virgin Nana, died by self-sacrifice under a pine-tree. Gautama the Buddha, son of Maya, attained his supreme Awakening as he sat in meditation beneath the Bo Tree. Odin learned the wisdom of the runes by immolating himself upon the World-Tree, Yggdrasil, with a spear cut from the same Tree:

> I know that I hung
> On a wind-rocked tree
> Nine whole nights,
> With a spear wounded,
> And to Odin offered
> Myself to myself;
> On that tree
> Of which no one knows
> From what root it springs.

In like manner, Adonis (= *Adonai*, the Lord) was born of Myrrha the myrtle, and the Babylonian god Tammuz was associated in his death with the cedar, the tamarisk, and the willow.

In almost all the mythological traditions this Tree is the *Axis Mundi*, the Centre of the World, growing in the "navel of the world" as, in medieval drawings, the Tree of Jesse is shown growing from the navel of Jesse. In the myth of Eden the Tree stands in the *centre* of the Garden, at the source of *four* rivers which "go out to water the garden".

from *Myth and Ritual in Christianity* by ALAN W. WATTS
(1915–1973)

The Human Tree

MANY have Earth's lovers been,
Tried in seas and wars, I ween;
Yet the mightiest have I seen:
    Yea, the best saw I.
One that in a field alone
Stood up stiller than a stone
    Lest a moth should fly.

Birds had nested in his hair,
On his shoon were mosses rare,
Insect empires flourished there,
    Worms in ancient wars;
But his eyes burn like a glass,
Hearing a great sea of grass
    Roar towards the stars.

From them to the human tree
Rose a cry continually,
'Thou art still, our Father, we
    Fain would have thee nod.
Make the skies as blood below thee,
Though thou slay us, we shall know thee.
    Answer us, O God!

'Show thine ancient fame and thunder,
Split the stillness once asunder,
Lest we whisper, lest we wonder
    Art thou there at all?'
But I saw him there alone,
Standing stiller than a stone
    Lest a moth should fall.

G. K. CHESTERTON (1874–1936)

The Tree

I STOOD still and was a tree amid wood,
Knowing the truth of things unseen before;
Of Daphne and the laurel bow
And that god-fearing couple old
That grew elm-oak amid the wold.
'Twas not until the gods had been
Kindly entreated, and been brought within
Unto the hearth of their heart's home
That they might do this wonder thing;
Nathless I have been a tree amid a wood
And many a new thing understood
That was rank folly to my head before.

EZRA POUND (1885–1972)

BEHOLD a tree. Outwardly it has a hard and rough
shell, appearing dead and encrusted; but the body
of the tree has a living power, which breaks through
the hard and dry bark and generates many young bodies,
branches, and leaves, which however, all are rooted
in the body of the tree. Thus it is with the whole
house of this world, wherein also the holy light of
God appears to have died out, because it has withdrawn
into its principle, and therefore it seems dead,
although it still exists in God. But love ever again
and again breaks through this very house of death and
generates holy and celestial branches in this great
tree, and which root in the light.

JACOB BOEHME (1575–1624)
from *Aurora*

As they entered the great forest, the Children stuck close together, with the Cat and the Dog on either side of them. They were awed by the silence and the darkness and they felt much relieved when the Cat exclaimed:

'Here we are! Turn the diamond!'

Then the light spread around them and showed them a wonderful sight. They were standing in the forest, where all the old, old Trees seemed to reach up to the sky. Wide avenues formed a white star amidst the dark green of the wood. Everything was peaceful and still; but suddenly a strange shiver ran through the foliage: the branches moved and stretched like human arms; the roots raised the earth that covered them, came together , took the shapes of legs and feet and stood on the ground; a tremendous crash rang through the air: the trunks of the Trees burst open and each of them let out its soul, which made its appearance like a funny human figure.

Some stepped slowly from their trunks; others came out with a jump; and all of them gathered inquisitively round our friends.

from *The Children's Blue Bird* by
GEORGETTE LEBLANC MAETERLINCK after the play
The Blue Bird by Maeterlinck (1862–1949)

"ARE you a dream?" he asked simply, having no words for his wonder.

"No, Cathal, I am no dream. I am a woman."

"A woman? But ... but ... you have no body as other women have: and I see the moonbeam that is on your breast shining upon the moss behind you!"

"Is it thinking you are, poor Cathal, that there are no women and no men in the world except those who are in thick flesh, and move about in the suntide?"

Cathal stared wonderingly.

"I am of the green people, Cathal. We are of the woods. I am a woman of the woods."

"Hast thou a name, fair woman?"

"I am called Deòin."

"That is well. Truly 'Green Breath' is a good name for thee. Are there others of thy kin in this place?"

"Look!" and at that she stooped, lifted the dew of a white flower in the moonshine, and put it upon his eyes.

Cathal looked about him. Everywhere he saw tall, fair pale-green lives moving to and fro: some passing out of trees, swift and silent as rain out of a cloud; some passing into trees, silent and swift as shadows. All were fair to look upon: tall, lithe, graceful, moving this way and that in the moonshine, pale green as the leaves of the lime, soft shining, with radiant eyes, and delicate earth-brown hair.

"Who are these, Deòin?" Cathal asked in a low whisper of awe.

"They are my people: the folk of the woods: the green people."

"But they come out of trees: they come and they go like bees in and out of a hive."

"Trees? That is your name for us of the woods. *We* are the trees."

"*You* the trees, Deòin! How can that be?"

"There is life in your body. Where does it go when the body sleeps, or when the sap rises no more to heart or brain, and there is chill in the blood, and it is like frozen water? Is there a life in your body?"

"Ay, so. I know it."

"The flesh is *your* body; the tree is *my* body."

"Then you are the green life of a tree?"

"I am the green life of a tree."

"And these?"

"They are as I am."

from *Cathal of the Woods,*
a legend by FIONA MACLEOD
(William Sharp – 1855–1905)

'Now are you two lawfully seized and possessed of all Old England,' began Puck, in a sing-song voice. 'By the right of Oak, Ash, and Thorn are you free to come and go and look and know where I shall show or best you please. You shall see What you shall see and you shall hear What you shall hear, though It shall have happened three thousand year; and you shall know neither Doubt nor Fear. Fast! Hold fast all I give you.' The children shut their eyes, but nothing happened. 'Well?' said Una, disappointedly opening them. 'I thought there would be dragons.'

from *Puck of Pook's Hill*
by RUDYARD KIPLING (1865–1936)

BUT the professore had gone, I am sorry to say, even further than that; for he had read at the British Association at Melbourne, Australia, in the year 1999, a paper which assured everyone who found himself the better or wiser for the news, that there were not, never had been, and could not be, any rational or half-rational beings except men, anywhere, anywhen, or anyhow; that nymphs, satyrs, fauns, inui, dwarfs, trolls, elves, gnomes, fairies, brownies, pixies, wilis, kobolds, leprechaunes, cluricaunes, banshees, will-o'-the-wisps, follets, luttins, magots, goblins, afrits, marids, jinns, ghouls, peris, deevs, angels, archangels, imps, bogies, or worse, were nothing at all, and pure bosh and wind . . .

. . . .

. . . .

"It is a water-baby!" cried Ellie; and of course it was. "Water-fiddlesticks, my dear!" said the professor; and he turned away sharply. There was no denying it. It was a water-baby: and he had said a moment ago that there were none. What was he to do?

from *The Water Babies* by
CHARLES KINGSLEY (1819–1875)

MY nurse used to tell me fairy tales, and I believed in ghosts, in fairies, in wood-demons, in every kind of monster. I remember well! I used to steal corrosive sublimate from father's room, sprinkle it on gingerbread, and leave it in the attic, so that the ghosts might eat it and die.

from *On the Way,* a short
story by ANTON CHEKHOV (1860–1904)

19

AT nightfall he brought them to his ent-house: nothing more than a mossy stone set upon turves under a green bank. Rowan-trees grew in a circle about it, and there was water (as in all ent-houses), a spring bubbling out from the bank. They talked for a while as darkness fell on the forest. Not far away the voices of the Entmoot could be heard still going on; but now they seemed deeper and less leisurely, and every now and again one great voice would rise in a high and quickening music, while all the others died away. But beside them Bregalad spoke gently in their own tongue, almost whispering, and they learned that he belonged to Skinbark's people, and the country they had lived had been ravaged. That seemed to the hobbits quite enough to explain his 'hastiness', at least in the matter of Orcs.

'There were rowan-trees in my home,' said Bregalad, softly and sadly, 'rowan-trees that took root when I was an Enting, many many years ago in the quiet of the world. The oldest was planted by the Ents to try and please the Entwives, but they looked at them and smiled and said that they knew where whiter blossom and richer fruit were growing. Yet there are no trees of all that race, the people of the Rose, that are so beautiful to me. And these grew and grew, till the shadow of each was like a green hall, and their red berries in the autumn were a burden, and a beauty and a wonder. Birds used to flock there. I like birds, even when they chatter, and the rowan has enough and to spare. But the birds became unfriendly and greedy and tore at the trees, and threw the fruit down and did not eat it. Then Orcs came with axes and cut down my trees. I came and called them by their long names, but they did not quiver, they did not hear or answer: they lay dead.

O Orofarnë, Lassemista, Carnimírië!
O rowan fair, upon your hair how white the blossom lay!
O rowan mine, I saw you shine upon a summer'd day,
Your rind so bright, your leaves so light, your voice
    so cool and soft:
Upon your head how golden-red the crown you bore
aloft!
O rowan dead, upon your head your hair is dry and grey;
Your crown is spilled, your voice is stilled for ever and
    a day.
O Orofarnë, Lassemista, Carnimírië!

The hobbits fell asleep to the sound of the soft singing of Bregalad, that seemed to lament in many tongues the fall of trees he had loved.

from *The Lord of the Rings* by J. R. R. TOLKIEN (1892–1973)

The Juniper Tree

A LONG while ago, perhaps as much as two thousand years, there was a rich man who had a wife of whom he was very fond; but they had no children. Now, in the garden before the house where they lived, there stood a juniper tree; and one winter's day as the lady was standing under the juniper tree, paring an apple, she cut her finger, and the drops of blood trickled down upon the snow. "Ah!" said she, sighing deeply, and looking down upon the blood, "how happy should I be if I had a little child as white as snow and as red as blood!" And as she was saying this she grew quite cheerful, and was sure her wish would be fulfilled. And after a little time the snow went away, and soon afterwards the fields began to look green. Next the spring came and the meadows were dressed with flowers; the trees put forth their green leaves; the young branches shed their blossoms upon the ground; and the little birds sang through the groves. And then came summer and the sweet smelling flowers of the juniper tree began to unfold; and the lady's heart leapt with her, and she fell on her knees for joy. But when autumn drew near the fruit was thick upon the trees. Then the lady plucked the red berries from the juniper tree, and looked sad and sorrowful; she called her husband to her, and said, "If I die, bury me under the juniper tree." Not long after this a pretty little child was born; it was, as the lady wished, as red as blood and as white as snow; and as soon as she had looked upon it, her joy overcame her, and she fainted away and died.

Then her husband buried her under the juniper tree, and wept and mourned over her; but after a little while he grew better, and at length dried up his tears and married another wife.

from a *Grimm's Fairy Tale* (first published 1812–15)

The Stolen Child

WHERE dips the rocky highland
    Of Sleuth Wood in the lake,
There lies a leafy island
    Where flapping herons wake
The drowsy water-rats.
There we've hid our fairy vats
Full of berries,
And of reddest stolen cherries.
Come away, O, human child!
To the woods and waters wild,
With a fairy hand in hand,
For the world's more full of weeping than
        you can understand.

Where the wave of moonlight glosses
    The dim grey sands with light,
Far off by furthest Rosses
    We foot it all the night,
Weaving olden dances,
Mingling hands, and mingling glances,
    Till the moon has taken flight;
To and fro we leap,
    And chase the frothy bubbles,
    While the world is full of troubles.
And is anxious in its sleep.
Come away! O, human child!
To the woods and waters wild,
With a fairy hand in hand,
For the world's more full of weeping than
        you can understand.

Where the wandering water gushes
    From the hills above Glen-Car,
In pools among the rushes,
    That scarce could bathe a star,
We seek for slumbering trout,
    And whispering in their ears;
      We give them evil dreams,
Leaning softly out
    From ferns that drop their tears
      Of dew on the young streams.
Come! O, human child!
To the woods and waters wild,
With a fairy hand in hand,
For the world's more full of weeping than
        you can understand.

Away with us, he's going,
    The solemn-eyed;
He'll hear no more the lowing
    Of the calves on the warm hill-side.
Or the kettle on the hob
    Sing peace into his breast;
Or see the brown mice bob
    Round and round the oatmeal chest.
For he comes, the human child,
To the woods and waters wild,
With a fairy hand in hand,
For the world's more full of weeping than
        he can understand.

W. B. YEATS (1865–1939)

I Bended unto Me

I BENDED unto me a bough of may,
That I might see and smell:
It bore it in a sort of way,
It bore it very well.
But when I let it backward sway,
Then it were hard to tell
With what a toss, with what a swing,
The dainty thing
Resumed its proper level,
And sent me to the devil.
I know it did - you doubt it?
I turned, and saw them whispering about it.

T. E. BROWN (1830–1897)

No one ever knew Susan's fears, she never even formulated them to herself, except as "things." But whether they were giants which she half expected to see straddle out of the dark distance, or dwarfs, hidden behind the trees, or bears and Indians in the undergrowth, or even the trees themselves marching down upon her, she was not certain. They must never be mentioned, and, above all, They must never know she was afraid.

It was no use for her to tell herself there were no giants, or that bears had disappeared in England centuries ago, or that trees could not walk. She knew that quite well, but the terror remained, a subconscious fear which quickly rose to consciousness when she pressed back the catch of the gate at the entrance to the wood, and closed it soundlessly, as she entered the deep listening wood on her way home from school in the dusky evenings.

In the middle of Dark Wood the climbing path rose up a steep incline, too steep for Susan to hurry, with black shadows on either side. Then it skirted a field, a small, queer, haunted-looking field of ragwort and bracken, long given back to the wild wood, which pressed in on every side. A high rudely-made wall surrounded it, through the chinks of which she was sure that eyes were watching. To pass this field was the culmination of agony, for she had to walk close to the wall in the semi-darkness of overhanging trees, and nothing could save her if a long arm and skinny hand shot out.

from *A Country Child*
by ALISON UTTLEY (1884–1976)

Tree that I Love

For L.D.

TREE that I love,
   tree in my likeness,
      so heavy with music
under the wind's fingers
   that turn your pages
      like a fairy tale,
     tree
        knowing like me
the voice of silence
   that sways
the depth of your green locks
   the quiver of your living hands
tree
   that I love
     my all alone
       lost like me
         lost in the sky
           lost in the mud
lacquered in dancing light
by the rain
tree
   echo of wind's grief
   and bird's joy
tree undressed by winter
for the first time I watch you.
Before, my eyes
    my ears
      knew you
or thought they knew you
   but they watched you alone.
Tonight,
   it is with a heart
of grey
   I look at you
the grey of what is already no more
   of ashes
the grey of the waves of the sky
the grey of the clouds of the sea
the silent grey
   of the motionless breast
     of a dead sparrow,
grey
   of the grey caressed with light
   in old soft pewter.
Tree like me
   wretched like me
     now like me
      only tense nerves
        against the grey sky
you are no longer a rounded head
   or a shape
but only
    the caricature
   of a big leaf

stripped of its blade
   by the cold,
a leaf
   whose every vein
     stretches its claw
       towards the sky.
Tree
    drawn by a clumsy
     child
a child too poor
   to buy
     coloured chalks
who scribbled you
with the brown left over
from his maps at school.
Tree I come to you
   console me
   for being only me.
With a light grey pussy-cat step
   the wind has risen
   a wind crowned
     with clouds
       of soft cotton wool
a wind
   with a pond-coloured skirt
and its prying fingers
   have ruffled the branches.
The sky has blossomed
   with light petals
   with twin petals
beating like wings
   and loud as the flap
     of a sail
the flight of blue pigeons
     fell like leaves
onto a naked branch
   like a cheek
   held up
   like a cheek
onto the branch dancing
     like a boat
which the tree
   the tree that I love
   suddenly
   unexplainedly
   so far away from me
   had offered
   as a woman
   offers her hand
which the tree
   had offered
to the coral feet
   of the blue pigeons
   perfumed with far away.

MINOU DROUET (b.1947)
(aged 8) translated from the French
by Margaret Crosland

Woods in Winter

WHEN winter winds are piercing chill,
    And through the hawthorn blows the gale,
With solemn feet I tread the hill
    That overbrows the lonely vale.

O'er the bare upland, and away
    Through the long reach of desert woods
The embracing sunbeams chastely play,
    And gladden these deep solitudes.

Where, twisted round the barren oak,
    The summer vine in beauty clung,
And summer winds the stillness broke,
    The crystal icicle is hung.

Where from their frozen urns, mute springs
    Pour out the river's gradual tide,
Shrilly the skater's iron rings,
    And voices fill the woodland side.

Alas! How changed from the fair scene,
    Where birds sang out their mellow lay,
And winds were soft, and woods were green,
    And the song ceased not with the day!

But still wild music is abroad,
    Pale desert woods! Within your crowd;
And gathering winds, in hoarse accord,
    Amid the vocal reeds pipe loud.

Chill airs and wintry winds! My ear
    Has grown familiar with your song;
I hear it in the opening year,
    I listen, and it cheers me long.

HENRY WADSWORTH LONGFELLOW (1807–1882)

You naked trees, whose shady leaves are lost,
Wherein the byrds were wont to build their bowre,
And now are clothd with mosse and hoary frost,
Instede of bloosmes, wherewith your buds did flowre;
   I see your teares that from your boughes doe raine,
   Whose drops in drery ysicles remaine.

   All so my lustful leafe is drye and sere,
My timely buds with wayling all are wasted;
The blossome which my braunch of youth did beare
With breathed sighes is blowne away and blasted;
   And from mine eyes the drizling teares descend,
As on your boughes the ysicles depend.

from *The Shepheardes Calender: Januarie*
by EDMUND SPENSER (1552–99)

IN the drear-nighted December,
    Too happy, happy tree,
Thy branches ne'er remember
    Their green felicity:
The north cannot undo them,
With a sleety whistle through them
Nor frozen thawings glue them
    From budding at the prime.

from *In a Drear-Nighted December*
by JOHN KEATS (1795–1821)

How different from this spring lyric is the epic of autumn – a west wind in the wood! The leaves have lost their individuality, like a multitude of people on some calamitous day. Wild and reckless companies fly down the rides, beech and hornbeam, elm, ash and sycamore, in strangely assorted crowds – no longer in demure families, each on its own tree. The sound of their hurrying feet comes near, then with wild unreason they turn, desperately flying from the invisible. Before the old west wind that blows from the sunset, the wise wind that knew the Atlantic before a ship was on it, the strong wind that maddens the sea-horses, it is no wonder that the leaves are afraid. The very trees are bending double before it, groaning in the agony of their defiance. The lithe birches sweep to earth in an ecstasy of surrender; the fir-trees lash themselves; the saplings have learnt obedience – their slender elasticity is at the wind's will; only the stiff old oaks and elms refuse to yield, and ominous crashes tell of their struggle. The live creatures of the wood have hidden from the tumult. The most living things in the place are the leaves; with their scurrying feet and their complaining, whispering voices, they are like an elfin nation, a lost tribe, a defeated army that has forgotten discipline. The sight and the sound of this world-old conflict brings the same strong exhilaration as music does, when it quickens and deepens to a climax.

from *Spring of Joy*
by MARY WEBB (1881–1927)

The Wind

THE wind,
It is a ghostly hand
Pushing to and fro
The leaves and stray paper
That lay scattered in his path.

The trees
Bow down to the strength
Of the whistling wind,
As though paying homage
To some unknown king.

N. CAREY (aged 11)
Poems by Children – Routledge & Kegan Paul, 1962

BUT little Boy Blue was not content,
Calling for followers still as he went,

Blowing his horn, and beating his drum,
And crying aloud, "Come all of you, come!"

He said to the shadows, "Come after me;"
And the shadows began to flicker and flee,

And they flew through the wood all flattering and fluttering,
Over the dead leaves flickering and muttering.

And he said to the wind, "Come, follow; come, follow,
With whistle and pipe, and rustle and hollo."

And the wind wound round at his desire,
As if he had been the gold cock on the spire.

And the cock itself flew down from the church
And left the farmers all in the lurch.

They run and they fly, they creep and they come,
Everything, everything, all and some.

The very trees they tugged at their roots,
Only their feet were too fast in their boots,

After him leaning and straining and bending,
As on through their boles he kept walking and wending,

Till out of the wood he burst on a lea,
Shouting and calling, "Come after me!"

And then they rose up with a leafy hiss,
And stood as if nothing had been amiss.

Little Boy Blue sat down on a stone,
And the creatures came round him every one.

from *At the Back of the North Wind*
by GEORGE MacDONALD (1824–1905)

November 1

THE fields to-day with a grey mist are fraught,
　　As though not all the ghosts went home last night
To neighbouring graveyards; some the spider caught
　　In his slung hammocks, where they glimmer white,
　　And some are trailing hence with the gold light
That drives them home. A birch stands lightly draped
　　With golden gauze that does not hide from sight
Her lithe white limbs, as delicately shaped
As those of fay or faun from elfin land escaped.

November 29

AND alders ring the bog, and bracken grows
　　Beside it and birch saplings, or a willow
Raises huge arms; there one might find repose
　　In any place, with heather for a pillow.
　　Some ancient lost thing, like an armadillo,
Might find a home there, so remote would seem
　　From all the busy earth the heather's billow
That ripples in mild winds, where mosses gleam
By pools that seem to touch earth's shores and those of
　　dream.

from *The Year*
by LORD DUNSANY (1878–1957)

Impermanence

SINCE that far day when Heaven and Earth were new,
Plain to mankind hath been the certainty
That this our world is all impermanence.
Gaze on the heavens, and mark the gleaming moon,
That ever waxes, evermore to wane.
The steep hillsides, tree-clad, flow'r-wreathed in Spring,
Are fair with blossom; but the Autumn comes,
The cold dew falls, and hoar-frosts' searing touch
Sets the hillside aflame with ruddy leaves—
The red leaf falls, and leaves the branches bare!
So with mankind. Too soon the youthful cheek
Loses its freshness, and the jetty hair
Changes its shining darkness into grey.
The smiling morn turns to the tearful eve,
As the wind blows, unseen of mortal eye.
As the tide flows, nor for an instant stays;
So all the things pass, and all are mutable,
And I—I weep, and cannot stay my tears!

a Japanese poem, mid 4th to
mid 8th C. (trans. by Clara A. Walsh)

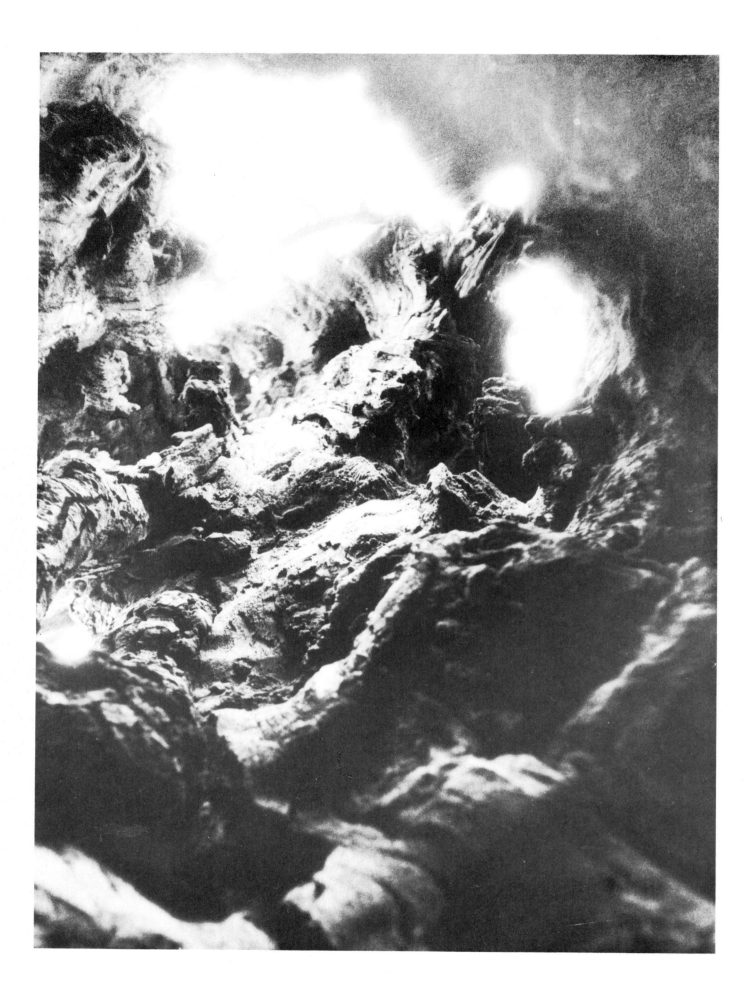

Pocket Magic

I HAVE a little acorn,
And nothing will it bear
But a giant oak tree
A-slumbering in there.

I keep it in my pocket,
Too small to hold a tree,
And wonder shall I plant it
To unfold its mystery.

But I love my little acorn,
And filled with adoration,
Grow the tree to its full height
In my imagination . . .

And wonder who first grew it so,
For me to follow later . . .?
It must have been a flicker
In the mind of the Creator.   HERBERT WHONE (1925–

The Timber

Sure thou didst flourish once! and many springs,
　Many bright mornings, much dew, many showers,
Pass'd o'er thy head; many light hearts and wings,
　Which now are dead, lodg'd in thy living bowers.

And still a new succession sings and flies;
　Fresh groves grow up, and their green branches shoot
Towards the old and still enduring skies,
　While the low violet thrives at their root.

But thou beneath the sad and heavy line
　Of death, doth waste all senseless, cold, and dark;
Where not so much as dreams of light may shine,
　Nor any thought of greenness, leaf, or bark.

And yet—as if some deep hate and dissent,
　Bred in thy growth betwixt high winds and thee,
Were still alive—thou dost great storms resent
　Before they come, and know'st how near they be.

Else all at rest thou liest, and the fierce breath
　Of tempests can no more disturb thy ease;
But this thy strange resentment after death
　Means only those who broke—in life—thy peace.

HENRY VAUGHAN 1622–1695

CH'ING, the chief carpenter, was carving wood into a stand for musical instruments. When finished, the work appeared to those who saw it as though of supernatural execution; and the Prince of Lu asked him, saying 'What mystery is there in your art?'

'No mystery, Your Highness,' replied Ch'ing. 'And yet there is something. When I am about to make such a stand, I guard against any diminution of my vital power. I first reduce my mind to absolute quiescence. Three days in this condition, and I become oblivious of any reward to be gained. Five days, and I become oblivious of any fame to be acquired. Seven days, and I become unconscious of my four limbs and my physical frame. Then, with no thought of the Court present in my mind, my skill becomes concentrated, and all disturbing elements from without are gone. I enter some mountain forest, I search for a suitable tree. It contains the form required, which is afterwards elaborated. I see the stand in my mind's eye, and then set to work. Beyond that there is nothing. I bring my own native capacity into relation with that of the wood. What was suspected to be of supernatural execution in my work was due solely to this.'

from the *Chuang Tzu*
(a collection of Taoist writings circa 300 B.C.)

Grow, my song, like a tree,
   And when I am grown old,
Let me die under thee,
   Die to enrich thy mould;
Die at thy roots, and so
   Help thee to grow.
Make of this body and blood
   Thy sempiternal food.
Then let some little child,
   Some friend I shall not see,
When the great dawn is gray,
   Some lover I have not known,
In summers far away,
   Sit listening under thee.
And in thy rustling hear
   That mystical undertone,
Which made my tears run wild,
   And made thee, O, how dear.

In the great years to be?
   I am proud then? Ah, not so.
I have lived and died for thee.
   Be patient. Grow.
Grow, my song, like a tree.

from *The Song-Tree*
by ALFRED NOYES (1880–1959)

Arbor Vitae

WITH honeysuckle, over-sweet, festoon'd;
With bitter ivy bound;
Terraced with funguses unsound;
Deform'd with many a boss
And closed scar, o'ercushion'd deep with moss;
Bunch'd all about with pagan mistletoe;
And thick with nests of the hoarse bird
That talks, but understands not his own word;
Stands, and so stood a thousand years ago,
A single tree.
Thunder has done its worst among its twigs,
Where the great crest yet blackens, never pruned,
But in its heart, alway
Ready to push new verdurous boughs, whene'er
The rotting saplings near it fall and leave it air,
Is all antiquity and no decay.
Rich, though rejected by the forest-pigs,
Its fruit, beneath whose rough, concealing rind
They that will break it find
Heart-succouring savour of each several meat,
And kernell'd drink of brain-renewing power,
With bitter condiment and sour,
And sweet economy of sweet,
And odours that remind
Of haunts of childhood and a different day.
Beside this tree,
Praising no Gods nor blaming, sans a wish,
Sits, Tartar-like, the Time's civility,
And eats its dead-dog off a golden dish.

COVENTRY PATMORE (1823–96)

The Trees

I DID not know your names and yet I saw
   The handiwork of Beauty in your boughs,
I worshipped as the Druids did, in awe,
   Feeling at Spring my pagan soul arouse
To see your leaf-buds open to the day,
   And dull green moss upon your ragged girth,
The hoary sanctity of your decay,
   Life and Death glimmering upon the Earth.

EDWARD L. DAVISON (pub. 1920)

A Hollow Wood

THIS is the mansion built for me
By the sweating centuries;
Roofed with intertwinèd tree,
Woofed with green for my princelier ease.
Here I lie with my world about me,
Shadowed off from the world without me,
Even as my thoughts embosom me
From wayside humanity.
And here can only enter who
Delight me—the unpricèd few.
Come you in, and make you cheer,
It draweth toward my banquet-time.
Would you win to my universe,
Your thought must turn in the wards of rhyme.
Loose the chain of linkèd verse,
Stoop your knowledge, and enter here!

Here cushioned ivies you invite
To fall to with appetite.
What for my viands?—Dainty thoughts.
What for my brows?—Forget-me-nots.
What for my feet?—A bath of green.
My servers?—Phantasies unseen.
What shall I find me for feasting dress?—
Your white disusèd childlikeness.
What hid music will laugh to my calls?—
An orgy of mad bird-bacchanals.
Such meat, such music, such coronals!
From the cask which the summer sets aflow
Under the roof of my raftered house,
The birds above, we below,
We carouse as they carouse.
Or have but the ear the ear within,
And you may hear, if you hold you mute,
You may hear by my amulet,
The wind-like keenness of violin,
The enamelled tone of shallow flute,
And the furry richness of clarinet.
These are the things shall make you cheer,
If you will grace my banquet-time.
Would you win to my universe,
Your thought must turn in the wards of rhyme.
Loose the chain of linkèd verse,
Steep your knowledge, and enter here!

FRANCIS THOMPSON (1859–1907)

THEY asked a philosopher, Why, when God Most High had
created so many famous fruitful trees, the cypress alone was
called free, which bore no fruit? and what was the meaning of
this? He replied "Every tree has its appointed time and season,
so that, during the said season, it flourishes; and when that is
past, it droops. But the cypress is not exposed to either of these
vicissitudes, and is at all times fresh and green; and this is the
condition of the free man".

from *The Gulistan* or *Rose Garden*
by SA'DI OF SHIRAZ (1193–1291)

FORM too possesses great importance, its importance residing
in the fact that it is associated with substance. Just as a thing
fails if it lacks a kernel, so too it fails if it lacks a skin. If you
sow a seed in the earth without its husk, it does not germinate,
whereas if you bury it in the earth it does germinate and
becomes a great tree. So from this viewpoint the body too is
a great and necessary principle, and without it the task fails and
the purpose is not attained.

from *The Discourses*
of JALAL AL-DIN RUMI (1207–1273)

NOW I am here, what thou wilt do with me
　　None of my books will show;
I reade, and sigh, and wish I were a tree;
　　For sure then I should grow
To fruit or shade: at least some bird would trust
Her household to me, and I should be just.

from *Affliction* by GEORGE HERBERT (1593–1633)

The little boy lost

THE wood was rather old and dark
The witch was very ugly
And if it hadn't been for father
Walking there so smugly
I never should have followed
The beckoning of her finger.
Ah me how long ago it was
And still I linger
Under the ever interlacing beeches
Over a carpet of moss.
I lift my hand but it never reaches
To where the breezes toss
The sun-kissed leaves above.
The sun?
Beware.
The sun never comes here.
Round about and round I go
Up and down and to and fro,
The woodlouse hops upon the tree
Or should do but I really cannot see.
Happy fellow. Why can't I be
Happy as he?
The wood grows darker every day
It's now a bad place in a way
But I lost the way
Last Tuesday.
Did I love father, mother, home?
Not very much; but now they're gone
I think of them with kindly toleration
Bred inevitably of separation.
Really if I could find some food
I should be happy enough in this wood
But darker days and hungrier I must spend
Till hunger and darkness make an end.

STEVIE SMITH (1902–1971)

46

THEN the pattering began.

He thought it was only falling leaves at first, so slight and delicate was the sound of it. Then as it grew it took a regular rhythm, and he knew it for nothing else but the pat-pat-pat of little feet, still a very long way off. Was it in front or behind? It seemed to be first one, then the other, then both. It grew and it multiplied, till from every quarter as he listened anxiously, leaning this way and that, it seemed to be closing in on him. As he stood still to hearken, a rabbit came running hard towards him through the trees. He waited, expecting it to slacken pace, or to swerve from him into a different course. Instead, the animal almost brushed him as it dashed past, his face set and hard, his eyes staring. 'Get out of this, you fool, get out!' The Mole heard him mutter as he swung round a stump and disappeared down a friendly burrow.

(continued on page 48)

The pattering increased till it sounded like sudden hail on the dry-leaf carpet spread around him. The whole wood seemed running now, running hard, hunting, chasing, closing in round something or – somebody? In panic he began to run aimlessly, he knew not whither. He ran up against things, he fell over things and into things, he darted under things and dodged round things. At last he took refuge in the deep dark hollow of an old beech tree, which offered shelter, concealment – perhaps even safety, but who could tell? Anyhow, he was too tired to run any further and could only snuggle down into the dry leaves which had drifted into the hollow and hope he was safe for the time. As he lay there panting and trembling, and listening to the whistlings and the patterings outside, he knew it at last, in all its fullness, that dread thing which other little dwellers in field and in hedgerow had encountered here, and known as their darkest moment – that thing which the Rat had vainly tried to shield him from – the Terror of the Wild Wood!

from *The Wind in the Willows*
by KENNETH GRAHAME (1859–1932)

The Elfin-Grove

"I HOPE," said a woodman one day to his wife, "that the children will not run into that fir-grove by the side of the river; who they are that have come to live there I cannot tell, but I am sure it looks more dark and gloomy than ever, and some queer-looking beings are to be seen lurking about it every night, as I am told." The woodman could not say that they brought any ill luck as yet, whatever they were; for all the village had thriven more than ever since they came; the fields looked gayer and greener, and even the sky was a deeper blue. Not knowing what to say of them, the farmer very wisely let his new friends alone, and in truth troubled his head very little about them.

That very evening little Mary and her playfellow Martin were playing at hide-and-seek in the valley. "Where can he be hid?" said she; "he must have gone into the fir-grove," and down she ran to look. Just then she spied a little dog that jumped round her and wagged his tail, and led her on towards the wood. Then he ran into it, and she soon jumped up the bank to look after him, but was overjoyed to see, instead of a gloomy grove of firs, a delightful garden, where flowers and shrubs of every kind grew upon turf of the softest green; gay butterflies flew about her, the birds sang sweetly, and, what was strangest, the prettiest little children sported about on all sides, some twining the flowers, and others dancing in rings upon the shady spots beneath the trees. In the midst, instead of the hovels of which Mary had heard, there was a palace that dazzled her eyes with its brightness. For a while she gazed on the fairy scene around her, till at last one of the little dancers ran up to her, and said, "And you are come at last to see us? we have often seen you play about, and wished to have you with us." Then she plucked some of the fruit that grew near; and Mary at the first taste forgot her home, and wished only to see and know more of her fairy friends.

Then they led her about with them and showed her all their sports. One while they danced by moonlight on the primrose banks; at another time they skipped from bough to bough among the trees that hung over the cooling streams; for they moved as lightly and easily through the air as on the ground; and Mary went with them everywhere, for they bore her in their arms wherever they wished to go. Sometimes they would throw seeds on the turf, and directly little trees sprang up: and then they would set their feet upon the branches, while the trees grew under them, till they danced upon the boughs in the air, wherever the breezes carried them; and again the trees would sink down into the earth and land them safely at their bidding. . . .

"And who are you?" said Mary one day. "We are what are called elves in your world," said one whose name was Gossamer, and who had become her dearest friend: "we are told you talk a great deal about us; some of our tribes like to work you mischief, but we who live here seek only to be happy: we meddle little with mankind; but when we do come among them, it is to do them good." "And where is your queen?" said little Mary. "Hush! hush! you cannot see or know her: you must leave us before she comes back, which will be now very soon, for mortal step cannot come where she is. But you will know that she is here when you see the meadows gayer, the rivers more sparkling, and the sun brighter".

The opening of *Grimm's Fairy Tale*

50

ONE glorious summer morning, when the wind and sun were out together, when the vanes were flashing, and the flags frolicking against the blue sky, little Daylight made her appearance from somewhere—nobody could tell where—a beautiful baby, with such bright eyes that she might have come from the sun, only by and by she showed such lively ways that she might equally well have come from out of the wind. There was great jubilation in the palace, for this was the first baby the queen had had, and there is as much happiness over a new baby in a palace as in a cottage.

But there is one disadvantage of living near a wood: you do not know quite who your neighbours may be. Everybody knew there were in it several fairies, living within a few miles of the palace, who always had had something to do with each new baby that came; for fairies live so much longer that we, that they can have business with a good many generations of human mortals. The curious houses they lived in were well known also,—one, a hollow oak; another, a birch-tree, though nobody could ever find how that fairy made a house of it; another, a hut of growing trees intertwined, and patched up with turf and moss. But there was another fairy who had lately come to the place, and nobody even knew she was a fairy except the other fairies. A wicked old thing she was, always concealing her power, and being as disagreeable as she could be, in order to tempt people to give her offence, that she might have the pleasure of taking vengeance upon them. The people about thought she was a witch, and those who knew her by sight were careful to avoid offending her. She lived in a mud house, in a swampy part of the forest.

from *At the Back of the North Wind*
by GEORGE MacDONALD (1824–1905)

It was perfectly still and presently the moon grew bright; if you had been there you would have seen the moonlight shining on an old tree-stump and on a fair-sized boulder. But if you had gone on looking you would gradually have begun to think there was something odd about both the stump and the boulder. And next you would have thought that the stump did look really remarkably like a little fat man crouching on the ground. And if you had watched long enough you would have seen the stump walk across to the boulder and the boulder sit up and begin talking to the stump; for in reality the stump and the boulder were simply the Witch and the dwarf. For it was part of her magic that she could make things look like what they aren't, and she had the presence of mind to do so at the very moment when the knife was knocked out of her hand. She had kept hold of her wand, so it had been kept safe, too.

from *The Lion, the Witch and the Wardrobe*
by C. S. LEWIS (1898–1963)

THE wood-demon of the Russians, Ljeschi, calls to mind both classical and modern tradition. He is of human form, with the horns, ears, and feet of a goat, his fingers are long claws, and he is covered with rough hair, often of a green colour. He can assume many forms, and vary his stature at will; in the fields he is no higher than the grass, in the woods as tall as the trees. Sometimes he is like a man, clothed in sheepskins, and often, like the cyclops, with only one eye. Like other wood demons, he announces his presence in the storm and the wind. He springs from tree to tree, and rocks himself in the branches, screeching and laughing, neighing, lowing and barking. He delights to mislead the traveller and plunge him in difficulties. However unfriendly to man Ljeschi is on good terms with animals; all the birds and beasts of the wood are under his protection, and the migrations of squirrels, field-mice, and such small deer are carried out under his guidance. The peasants are at pains to propitiate him. In the province of Olonitz the shepherds offer him a cow every summer, to secure his favour for the herd; elsewhere the hunter gives him the first thing he shoots, leaving it for him in an oak-wood, or places a piece of bread or pancake strewed with salt upon a tree-stump. There are certain ways of conjuring his presence and his aid by means of birch-twigs, or by muttering a given formula while standing on a tree-stump. . . .

from *The Sacred Tree*
by Mrs J. H. PHILPOTS (pub. 1897)

THE damsel had disappeared; but, in the shrubbery at the mouth of the cave, stood a strange, horrible object. It looked like an open coffin set up at one end, only that the part for the head and neck was defined from the shoulder-part. In fact it was a rough presentation of the human frame, only hollow, as if made of decaying bark torn from a tree. It had arms, which were only slightly seamed, down from the shoulder-blade by the elbow, as if the bark had healed again from the cut of a knife. But the arms moved, and the hands and fingers were tearing asunder a long, silky tress of hair. The thing turned round; it had for a face and front those of an enchantress, but now of a pale greenish hue in the light of the morning, and with dead, lusterless eyes. In the horror of the moment another fear invaded me. I put my hand to my waist; and found indeed that my girdle of beech-leaves was gone. Hair again in her hands, she was tearing it fiercely. Once more, as she turned, she laughed a low laugh, but now full of scorn and derision; and then she said, as if to a companion with whom she had been talking while I slept, "There he is; you can take him now."

I lay still, petrified with dismay and fear, for I now saw another figure beside her, which although vague and indistinct, I yet recognised but too well. It was the Ash-tree. My beauty was the Maid of the Alder! and she was giving me, spoiled of my only availing defense, into the hands of my foe. The Ash bent his gorgon-head, and entered the cave. I could not stir. He drew near me. His ghoul-eyes and his ghastly face fascinated me. He came stooping with the hideous hand outstretched, like a beast of prey. I had given myself up to a death of unfathomable horror, when, suddenly, and just as he was on the point of seizing me, the dull, heavy blow of an axe echoed through the forest, followed by others in quick repetition. The Ash shuddered and groaned, withdrew the outstretched hand, retreated backwards to the mouth of the cave, then turned and disappeared amongst the trees. The other walking Death looked at me once, with a careless dislike on her beautifully molded features; then, heedless any more to conceal her hollow deformity, turned her frightful back and likewise vanished amid the green obscurity without. I lay and wept. The Maid of the Alder-tree had befooled me – nearly slain me – in spite of all the warnings I had received from those who knew my danger.

from *Phantastes*
by GEORGE MacDONALD (1824–1905)

THE mourning birds wept for thee, Orpheus, the throng of beasts, the flinty rocks, and the trees which had so often gathered to thy songs; yes, the trees shed their leaves as if so tearing their hair in grief for thee. They say that the rivers also were swollen with their own tears, and that naiads and dryads alike mourned with dishevelled hair and with dark-bordered garments. The poet's limbs lay scattered all around; but his head and lyre, O Hebrus, thou didst receive, and (a marvel!) while they floated in mid-stream the lyre gave forth some mournful notes, mournfully the lifeless tongue murmured, mournfully the banks replied. And now, borne onward to the sea, they left their native stream and gained the shore of Lesbos near the city of Methymna. Here, as the head lay exposed upon a foreign strand, a savage serpent attacked it and its streaming locks still dripping with the spray. But Phoebus at last appeared, drove off the snake just in the act to bite, and hardened and froze to stone, just as they were, the serpent's widespread, yawning jaws.

The poet's shade fell beneath the earth, and recognised all the places he had seen before; and seeking through the blessed fields, found Eurydice and caught her in his eager arms. Here now side by side they walk; now Orpheus follows her as she precedes, now goes before her, now may in safety look back upon his Eurydice.

However, Lyaeus did not suffer such crime as this to go unavenged. Grieved at the loss of the bard of his sacred rites, he straightway bound fast all those Thracian women, who saw the impious deed, with twisted roots. For he prolonged their toes and, in so far as each root followed down, he thrust their tips into the solid earth. And as a bird, when it has caught its foot in the snare which the cunning fowler has set for it, and feels that it is caught, flaps and flutters, but draws its bonds tighter by its struggling; so, as each of these women, fixed firmly in the soil, had stuck fast, with wild affright, but all in vain, she attempted to flee. The tough roots held her, and though she struggled, kept firm their grasp. And when she asked where were her fingers, where her feet, her nails, she saw the bark come creeping up her shapely legs; striving to smite her thighs with hands of grief, she smote an oak. Her breasts also became of oak; oaken her shoulders. Her arms you would think had been changed to long branches – nor would your thought be wrong.

from *Metamorphoses Book XI*
by OVID (43B.C.–A.D.17)

It is thousands of years since Epimetheus and Pandora were alive; and the world, now-a-days, is a very different sort of thing from what it was in their time. Then, everybody was a child. There needed no fathers and mothers to take care of the children; because there was no danger or trouble of any kind, and no clothes to be mended, and there was always plenty to eat and drink. Whenever a child wanted his dinner, he found it growing on a tree: and, if he looked at the tree in the morning, he could see the expanding blossom of that night's supper; or, at eventide, he saw the tender bud of tomorrow's breakfast. It was a very pleasant life indeed. . . .

from *A Wonder Book* (The Paradise of Children)
by NATHANIEL HAWTHORNE (1804–1864)

The Sugar-Plum Tree

HAVE you ever heard of the Sugar-Plum Tree?
   'Tis a marvel of great renown!
It blooms on the shore of the Lollipop sea
   In the garden of Shut-Eye Town;
The fruit that it bears is so wondrously sweet
   (As those who have tasted it say)
That good little children have only to eat
   Of that fruit to be happy next day.

When you've got to the tree, you would have a hard time
   To capture the fruit which I sing;
The tree is so tall that no person could climb
   To the boughs where the sugar-plums swing.
But up in that tree sits a chocolate cat,
   And a gingerbread dog prowls below—
And this is the way you contrive to get at
   Those sugar-plums tempting you so:

You say but the word to that gingerbread dog
   And he barks with such terrible zest
That the chocolate cat is at once all agog,
   As her swelling proportions attest.
And the chocolate cat goes cavorting around
   From this leafy limb unto that,
And the sugar-plums tumble, of course, to the ground—
   Hurrah for that chocolate cat!

There are marshmallows, gumdrops, and peppermint canes,
   With stripings of scarlet or gold,
And you carry away of the treasure that rains
   As much as your apron can hold!
So come, little child, cuddle closer to me
   In your dainty white nightcap and gown,
And I'll rock you away to that Sugar-Plum Tree
   In the garden of Shut-Eye Town.

EUGENE FIELD (1850–1895)

The Holly

THE sturdiest of forest-trees
With acorns is inset;
Wan white blossoms the elder brings
To fruit as black as jet;
But O, in all green English woods
Is aught so fair to view
As the sleek, sharp, dark-leaved holly tree
And its berries burning through?

Towers the ash; and dazzling green
The larch her tassels wears;
Wondrous sweet are the clots of may
The tangled hawthorn bears;
But O, in heath or meadow or wold
Springs aught beneath the blue
As brisk and trim as a holly-tree bole
With its berries burning through?

When hither, thither, falls the snow,
And blazes small the frost,
Naked amid the winter stars
The elm's vast boughs are tossed;
But O, of all that summer showed
What now to winter's true
As the prickle-beribbed dark holly tree,
With its berries burning through!

WALTER de la MARE (1873–1956)

Holly Song from *As You Like It*

BLOW, blow, thou winter wind,
    Thou art not so unkind
        As man's ingratitude;
    Thy tooth is not so keen,
    Because thou art not seen,
        Although thy breath be rude.
Heigh, ho! sing, heigh, ho! unto the green holly:
Most friendship is feigning, most loving mere folly:
        Then, heigh, ho! the holly!
        This life is most jolly.

    Freeze, freeze, thou bitter sky,
    That dost not bite so nigh
        As benefits forgot:
    Though thou the waters warp,
    Thy sting is not so sharp,
        As friend remember'd not.
Heigh, ho! sing, heigh, ho! unto the green holly:
Most friendship is feigning, most loving mere folly:
        Then, heigh, ho! the holly!
        This life is most jolly.

WILLIAM SHAKESPEARE 1564–1616

Love and Friendship

LOVE is like the wild rose-brier;
    Friendship like the holly-tree.
The holly is dark when the rose-brier blooms,
    But which will bloom most constantly?

The wild rose-brier is sweet in spring,
    Its summer blossoms scent the air;
Yet wait till winter comes again,
    And who will call the wild-brier fair?

Then, scorn the silly rose-wreath now,
    And deck thee with the holly's sheen,
That, when December blights thy brow,
    He still may leave thy garland green.

EMILY BRONTË (1818–1848)

THE Dedannans had for food during the game, and for their journey afterwards, crimson nuts and arbutus apples and scarlet quicken berries, which they had brought from the Land of Promise. These fruits were gifted with many secret virtues; and the Dedannans were careful that neither apple nor nut berry should touch the soil of Erin. But as they passed through the Wood of Dooros, in Hy Ficra of the Moy, one of the scarlet quicken berries dropped on the earth; and the Dedannans passed on, not heeding.

From this berry a great quicken tree† sprang up, which had the virtues of the quicken trees that grow in Fairyland. For its berries had the taste of honey, and those who ate of them felt a cheerful flow of spirits, as if they had drunk of wine or old mead; and if a man were even a hundred years old, he returned to the age of thirty, as soon as he had eaten three of them.

Now when the Dedannans heard of this tree, and knew of its many virtues, they would not that any one should eat of the berries but themselves; and they sent a Fomor‡ of their own people to guard it, namely, Sharvan the Surly, of Lochlann; so that no man dared even to approach it. For this Sharvan was a giant of the race of the wicked Cain, burly and strong; with heavy bones, large, thick nose, crooked teeth, and one broad, red fiery eye in the middle of his black forehead. And he had a great club tied by a chain to an iron girdle which was round his body. He was, moreover, so skilled in magic that fire could not burn him, water could not drown him, and weapons could not wound him; and there was no way to kill him but by giving him three blows of his own club. By day he sat at the foot of the tree, watching; and at night he slept in a hut he had made for himself, high up among the branches.

from *Old Celtic Romances*
trans. by P. W. Joyce (1827–1914)

†a rowan
‡a giant

LEANING out over
The dreadful precipice,
One contemptuous tree.

from *Symmetries and Asymmetries*
by W. H. AUDEN (1907–1973)

Winter Branches

No one marvels when the tall
Oak resigns its leafy pall,
Yet only custom blinds our eyes,
And robs our hearts of shocked surprise.

Skeletons, dry bones and bare,
Are those boughs that prick the air—
Suppose all creatures bared their bones
To stand as winter skeletons?

If they did, and if we all
Doffed the body's living pall
In annual death, we should not be
More strange than that denuded tree.

No one wonders at the sight
Of its ribs against the light,
Yet only custom year on year
Has robbed our hearts of awe and fear.

ALBERTA VICKRIDGE (1890–1963)

Frozen Rain

MOURN for the tree that through a century
    Had garnered sun and rain, and from its store
Had builded up, with wizard alchemy,
    A thing so lovely that with all his love
Man could not fashion anything so fair!

Mourn, for one night of wind, and driving rain
    Caught in the cruel fingers of the frost,
Laid such a burden that, bowed low with pain,
    The tree was riven and the beauty lost;
One crippled bough thrust starkly into air
    All that the wind and weight of ice had left.
Mourn for the tree that through a century
    Had sheltered man and beast, and now is reft.

M. H. NOËL-PATON (pub. 1934)

Unseen Buds

UNSEEN buds, infinite, hidden well,
Under the snow and ice, under the darkness, in every square
   or cubic inch,
Germinal, exquisite, in delicate lace, microscopic, unborn,
Like babies in wombs, latent, folded, compact, sleeping;
Billions of billions, and trillions of trillions of them waiting,
(On earth and in the sea—the universe—the stars there in
   the heavens,)
Urging slowly, surely forward, forming endless,
And waiting ever more, forever more behind.

WALT WHITMAN (1819–1892)

A Backward Spring

THE trees are afraid to put forth buds,
And there is timidity in the grass;
The plots lie gray where gouged by spuds;
    And whether next week will pass
Free of sly sour winds is the fret of each bush
    Of barberry waiting to bloom.

Yet the snowdrop's face betrays no gloom,
And the primrose pants in its heedless push,
Though the myrtle asks if it's worth the fight
    This year with frost and rime
    To venture one more time
On delicate leaves and buttons of white
From the selfsame bough as at last year's prime,
And never to ruminate on or remember
What happened to it in mid-December.

THOMAS HARDY (1840–1928)

NATURE – sometimes sears a Sapling –
Sometimes – scalps a Tree –
Her Green People recollect it
When they do not die –

Fainter Leaves – to Further Seasons –
Dumbly testify –
We – who have the Souls –
Die oftener – Not so vitally –

EMILY DICKINSON (1830–1886)

The Trees of the Garden

YE who have passed Death's haggard hills; and ye
   Whom trees that knew your sires shall cease to know
   And still stand silent:——is it all a show,——
A wisp that laughs upon the wall?——decree
Of some inexorable supremacy
   Which ever, as man strains his blind surmise
   From depth to ominous depth, looks past his eyes,
Sphinx-faced with unabashèd augury?

Nay, rather question the Earth's self. Invoke
   The storm-felled forest-trees moss-grown to-day
   Whose roots are hillocks where the children play;
Or ask the silver sapling 'neath what yoke
   Those stars, his spray-crown's clustering gems, shall wage
   Their journey still when his boughs shrink with age.

Sonnet LXXXIX
by DANTE GABRIEL ROSSETTI
(1828–82)

A Dumb Friend

I PLANTED a young tree when I was young:
But now the tree is grown and I am old:
There wintry robin shelters from the cold
    And tunes his silver tongue.

A green and living tree I planted it,
A glossy-foliaged tree of evergreen:
All through the noontide heat it spread a screen
    Whereunder I might sit.

But now I only watch it where it towers:
I, sitting by my window, watch it tost
By rattling gale or silvered by the frost;
    Or, when sweet summer flowers,

Wagging its round green head with stately grace
In tender winds that kiss it and go by.
It shows a green full age: and what show I?
    A faded wrinkled face.

So often have I watched it, till mine eyes
Have filled with tears and I have ceased to see,
That now it seems a very friend to me,
    In all my secrets wise.

A faithful pleasant friend, who year by year
Grew with my growth and strengthened with my strength,
But whose green lifetime shows a longer length:
    When I shall not sit here.

It still will bud in spring, and shed rare leaves
In autumn, and in summer heat give shade,
And warmth in winter: when my bed is made
    In shade the cypress weaves.

CHRISTINA ROSSETTI (1830–1894)

January 23

ROADS are all ice; duck are in little streams;
    A starling in the powdery snow lies dead;
A mist has risen high and the sun gleams
    A disk of silver through; cattle are fed
    With hay thrown down where the smooth snow is spread
Over all else; rabbits look large and dark;
    No birds are singing, and a hush is shed
Over a white world which, for all we mark,
Might be a world at peace; and all the trees are stark.

January 24

NOW upon all the branches, twigs and sprays
    Have bloomed the ferny crystals of the frost,
And light is from the ground, for in a haze
    The sun and the increasing moon are lost.
    The sky is grey, but where its arch is crossed
By any trees, whose pallid clusters stand
    Against the darkness like a wandering ghost
Upon the edge of night, as the command
Of cockcrow turns him back into the lone dark land.

from *The Year* (1945)
by LORD DUNSANY (1878–1957)

The Girt Woak Tree

THE girt woak tree that's in the dell!
There's noo tree I doo love so well;
Vor times an' times when I wer young,
I there've a climb'd an' there've a-zwung,
An' pick'd the äcorns green, ashead
In wrestlèn storms vrom his broad head.
An' down below's the cloty brook
Wher I did vish with line an' hook,
An' beät, in plaÿsome dips an' zwims,
The foamy stream wi' white-skinn'd lim's.
An' there my mother nimbly shot
Her knittèn-needles, as she zot
At evenèn down below the wide
Woak's head, wi' father at her zide.
An' I've a-plaÿed wi' many a bwoy,
That's now a man an' gone awoy;
   Zoo I do like noo tree so well
    'S the girt woak tree that's in the dell.

An' there, in leäter years, I roved
Wi' thik poor maïd I fondly lov'd,
The maïd too feäir to die so soon,—
When evenèn twilight, or the moon,
Cast light enough 'ithin the pleäce
To show the smiles upon the feäce,
Wi' eyes so clear's the glassy pool,
An' lips an' cheäks so soft as wool.
There han' in han', wi' bosoms warm,
Wi' love that burn'd but thought noo harm,
Below the wide-bough'd tree we past
The happy hours that went too vast:
An' though she'll never be my wife,
She's still my leäden star o' life.
She's gone: an' she've a-left to me
Her mem'ry in the girt woak tree;
   Zoo I doo love noo tree so well
    'S the girt woak tree that's in the dell.

An' Oh! mid never ax nor hook
Be brought to spweil his steätely look;
Nor ever roun' his Rribby zides
Mid cattle rub ther heäiry hides;
Nor pigs rout up his turf, but keep
His lwonesome sheäde vor harmless sheep;
An' let 'en grow, an' let 'en spread,
An' let en live when I be dead.
But Oh! if men shou'd come an' vell
The girt woak tree that's in the dell,
An' build his planks 'ithin the zide
O' some girt ship to plow the tide,
Then, life or death! I'd goo to sea,
A-säilen wi' the girt woak tree:
An' I upon his planks would stand,
An' die a-fightèn vor the land,—
The land so dear,—the land so free,—
The land that bore the girt woak tree;
   Vor I doo love noo tree so well
    'S the girt woak tree that's in the dell.

line 7: Cloty = Water-lilied.

WILLIAM BARNES (1801–1886)

THOU wast a bauble once; a cup and ball,
Which babes might play with; and the thievish jay,
Seeking her food, with ease might have purloined
The auburn nut that held thee, swallowing down
Thy yet close-folded latitude of boughs,
And all thine embryo vastness, at a gulp.
But fate thy growth decreed; autumnal rains
Beneath thy parent tree mellowed the soil,
Designed thy cradle; and a skipping deer,
With pointed hoof dibbling the glebe, prepared
The soft receptacle, in which, secure,
Thy rudiments should sleep the winter through.

   So fancy dreams. Disprove it, if ye can,
Ye reasoners broad awake, whose busy search
Of argument, employed too oft amiss,
Sifts half the pleasures of short life away!

   Thou fell'st mature; and in the loamy clod
Swelling with vegetative force instinct
Didst burst thine egg, as theirs the fabled Twins,

Now stars; two lobes, protruding, paired exact;
A leaf succeeded, and another leaf,
And, all the elements thy puny growth
Fostering propitious, thou becamest a twig.

         . . . .

Thought cannot spend itself, comparing still
The great and little of thy lot, thy growth
From almost nullity into a state
Of matchless grandeur, and declension thence,
Slow, into such magnificent decay.
Time was when, settling on thy leaf, a fly
Could shake thee to the root – and time has been
When tempests could not.

excerpts from *Yardley Oak*
by WILLIAM COWPER (1731–1800)

The Round Oak

THE apple top't oak in the old narrow lane
And the hedge row of bramble and thorn
Will ne'er throw their green on my visions again
As they did on that sweet dewy morn
When I went for spring pooteys and birds nest to look
Down the border of bushes ayont the fair spring
I gathered the palm grass close to the brook
And heard the sweet birds in thorn bushes sing

I gathered flat gravel stones up in the shallows
To make ducks and drakes when I got to a pond
The reed sparrows nest it was close to the sallows
And the wrens in a thorn bush a little beyond
And there did the stickleback shoot through the pebbles
As the bow shoots the arrow quick darting unseen
Till it came to the shallows where the water scarce drebbles
Then back dart again to the spring head of green

The nest of the magpie in the low bush of white thorn
And the carrion crows nest on the tree o'er the spring
I saw it in march on many a cold morn
When the arum it bloomed like a beautiful thing
And the apple top't oak aye as round as a table
That grew just above on the bank by the spring
Where every saturday noon I was able
To spend half a day and hear the birds sing

But now there's no holidays left to my choice
That can bring time to sit in thy pleasures again
Thy limpid brook flows and thy waters rejoice
And I long for that tree—but my wishes are vain
All thats left to me now I find in my dreams
For fate in my fortune's left nothing the same
Sweet Apple top't oak that grew by the stream
I loved thy shade once now I love but thy name

JOHN CLARE (1793–1864)
written in Northampton asylum 1846
– original spelling and punctuation

THERE is a good deal of confusion in people's minds as to the right name for this familiar tree. Sycamore is not an English word, but is made from a Greek word meaning fig or mulberry. The tree has been so called because many years ago people believed that it was a relation of the fig tree which grows so abundantly by the roadside in Palestine. The leaves are a little alike, but there is no real resemblance between our English Great Maple and the Eastern Sycamore: the name has been given by mistake.

from *Trees Shown to the Children*
by J. H. KELMAN and C. E. SMITH

THE gods shall say unto me, "What manner of food wouldst thou have given unto thee?" (And I reply) "Let me eat my food under the sycamore tree of my lady the goddess Hathor, and let my times be among the divine beings who have alighted thereon."

from the *Egyptian Book of the Dead*

The Sycamore Tree

THERE was a Boy, long years ago,
That climbed a sycamore tree,
On the sun-kissed, wind-swept, last of land,
Between the hills and the sea.

The Boy went out, with the youth of the world,
From peace to the raging years,
To pain, and terror, and loneliness,
Hunger and thirst, and tears.

The Boy came back from a barren world,
Hatred, and blood, and strife,
And found his way to the sycamore tree,
As he groped for a faith in life.

The sycamore tree was standing , still,
Happy in summer leaf;
Her wise heart yearned to the pain of youth;
Her soft voice sang to his grief.

She told him the bluebells came with Spring;
The birds had followed the plough;
She showed him the rose and the woodbine wreaths
That twined on the hawthorn bough.

There was a Boy, but yesterday,
That climbed a sycamore tree,
And found the peace of a loved, lost world,
Between the hills and the sea.

F. E. STUTCHBURY (pub. 1947)

The Tree

I AM the great tree over above this house!
I resemble
The drawing of a tree. Drawing Just a Tree,
The child draws Me!
I am more old than the house is old.
I have known nights so cold
I used to tremble.
For the sap was frozen in my branches
And the mouse
That stored her nuts in my knot-holes, died. I am strong
Now. Let the storm come wild over the Sussex Wold,
I do not fear it.
I have stood too long.

from *A House*
by FORD MADOX FORD (1873–1939)

The Birch

THE birch grew weary of her leaves
And shed them on the sward,
And danced in naked loveliness
Before the sun, her lord—

And as that blue October day
She danced and waved to him
He gilded with his loving light
Each glancing naked limb.

WILFRID GIBSON (1878–1962)

Trees

THEY ask me where the Temple stands,
    And is the Abbey far from there;
They ask the way to old St. Paul's,
    And where they'll find Trafalgar Square.

As I pass on with my one thought
    To find a quiet place with trees,
I answer him, I answer her,
    I answer one and all of these.

When I sit under a green tree,
    Silent, and breathing all the while
As easy as a sleeping child,
    And smiling with a sort of smile—

Then, as my brains begin to work,
    This is the thought that comes to me,
Were such a peace more often mine,
    I'd live as long as this green tree.

W. H. DAVIES (1871–1940)

84

THE tree which moves some to tears is in the eyes
of others only a green thing which stands in the way.

WILLIAM BLAKE (1757–1827)
from a letter

Tree Names

In conclusion, a few words must be said about tree names, so common in their simple form and in topographical compounds. Here, as in the case of most of the etymons already mentioned in this chapter, the origin of the surname may be specific as well as general, i.e. the name *Ash* may come from Ash in Kent rather than from any particular tree, the etymology remaining the same. Many of our surnames have preserved the older forms of tree names, e.g. the *lime* was once the *line*, hence *Lines*, *Lymes*, and earlier still the *Lind*, as in the compounds *Lyndhurst*, *Lindley*, etc. The older form of *Oak* appears in *Acland*, *Acton*, and variants in *Ogden* and *Braddock*, broad oak. We have ash in *Aston*, and *Ascham*. The holly was once the *hollin*, whence *Hollins*, *Hollis*, and *Hollings*; c.f. *Hollingshead*, *Hollinshead*. But *hollins* became colloquially *holm* whence generally *Holmes*. *Homewood* is for holmwood. The holm oak, Ilex, is so called from its holly-like leaves. For *Birch* we also find *Birk*, a northern form. *Beech* often appears in compounds as *Buck*; cf *buckwheat*, so called because the grains are of the shape of beech-mast. In *Poppleton*, *Popplewell*, we have the dialect *popple*, a poplar. *Yeo* sometimes represents *yew*, spelt *yowe* in Palsgrave.

In *Sallows* we have a provincial name for the willow, cognate with Fr. *saule* and Latin *salix*. Rowntree is the *rowan*, or mountain ash, and *Bawtry* or *Bawtree* is a northern name for the elder. The older forms of *Alder* and *Elder*, in both of which the 'd' is intrusive appear in *Allerton* and *Ellershaw*. *Maple* is sometimes *Mapple* and *sycamore* is corrupted into *Sicklemore*.

Tree names are common in all languages. *Beerbolm Tree* is pleonastic, from German *Bierbaum*, for *Birnbaum*, pear-tree. A few years ago a prominent Belgian statesman bore the name of *Vandenpereboom*, rather terrifyingly till decomposed into 'van den pere boom'. Its mid. English equivalent appears in *Pirie*, originally a collection of pear-trees, but used by Chaucer for a single tree –

"And thus I lete hym sitte upon the pyrie."

From tree we may descend gradually, via *Thorne*, *Bush*, *Furze*, *Gorst* and *Ling*, etc., until we come finally to *Grace*, which in some cases represents grass, for we find William *atte grase* in 1327, while the name *Poorgrass*, in Mr Hardy's *Far From the Madding Crowd*, seems to be certified by the famous French names *Malherbe* and *Malesherbes*. But *Savory* is the French personal name *Savary*.

The following list of trees is given by Chaucer in the *Knight's Tale* –

"The names that the trees highte –
as ook, firre, birch, aspe, alder, holm, popeler,
Wylugh, elm, plane, asshe, box, chasteyn, lynde, laurel,
Mapul, thorn, bech, hasel, ew, whippeltre."

They are all represented in modern directories.

from *The Romance of Names*
by ERNEST WEEKLEY (1865–1954)

THOUGH rough-shaped by the wind,
all that shall be fulfilled
for the opportune weed
is immured in its seed:

if only I could take
the secret of the oak
from the acorn/ or learn
the nature of man from the head of a sperm!

GLYN HUGHES (1935–

A Seed

SEE how a seed, which Autumn flung down,
   And through the Winter neglected lay,
Uncoils two little green leaves and two brown,
   With tiny root taking hold on the clay.
   As, lifting and strengthening day by day,
It pushes red branchlets, sprouts new leaves,
And cell after cell the Power in it weaves
Out of the storehouse of soil and clime,
To fashion a Tree in due course of time;
Tree with rough bark and bough's expansion,
Where the Crow can build his mansion,
Or a Man, in some new May,
Lie under whispering leaves and say,
"Are the ills of one's life so very bad
When a Green Tree makes me deliciously glad?"
As I do now. But where shall I be
When this little Seed is a tall green Tree?

WILLIAM ALLINGHAM (1825–1888)

In a Myrtle Shade

WHY should I be bound to thee,
O my lovely Myrtle-tree?
Love, free Love, cannot be bound
To any tree that grows on ground.

O! how sick and weary I
Underneath my Myrtle lie;
Like to dung upon the ground,
Underneath my Myrtle bound.

Oft my Myrtle sigh'd in vain
To behold my heavy chain:
Oft my Father saw us sigh,
And laugh'd at our simplicity.

So I smote him, and his gore
Stain'd the roots my Myrtle bore.
But the time of youth is fled,
And grey hairs are on my head.

WILLIAM BLAKE (1757–1827)
a poem from the Rossetti ms

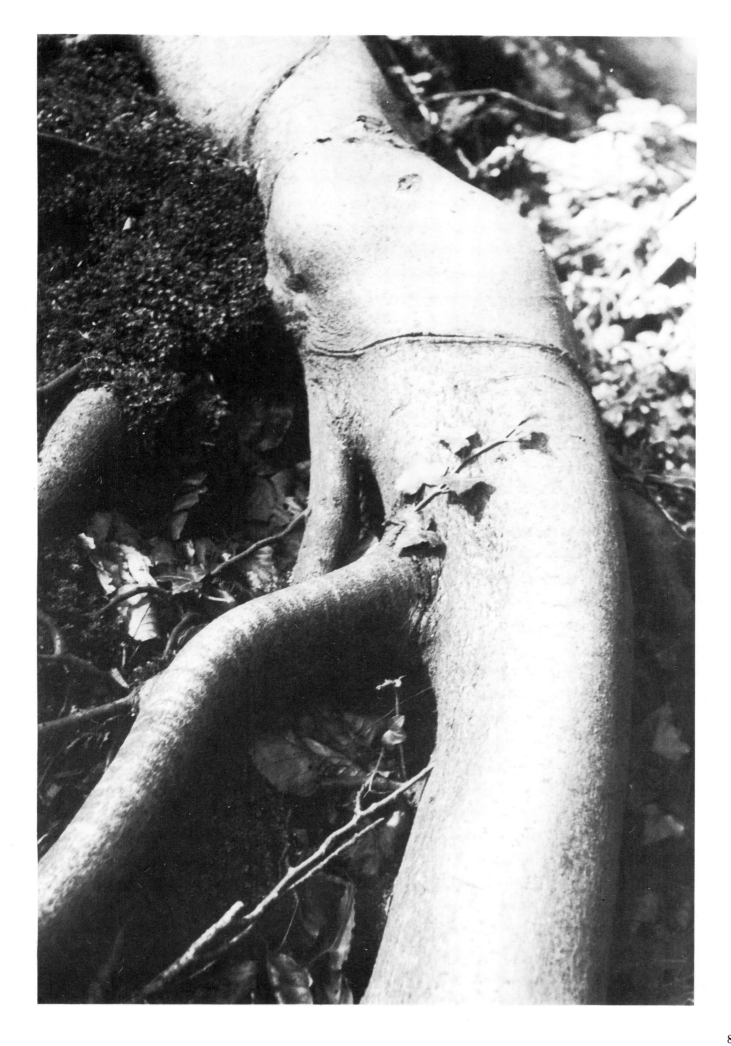

No young leaves are more interesting than those of the horse-chestnut, which every lover of nature who passes the spring in the country must have watched daily in April, if the tree happened to grow within a little distance of his residence. When they get fairly out of the cotton, in which they have been so snugly protected against the severities of the early season, they first hang straight down in the most languid manner, and it is only after many days that they begin to spread themselves in the air like the fingers of an extended hand. No leaf but that of the beech looks *newer* than the young horse-chestnut. There is a great difference amongst trees in this respect, for some young leaves have a very old look indeed, and might be taken by a half-observant person for remnants of the later year; but when the horse-chestnut leaf is young, it has that air of newness which is seen in human work that has just left the hands of the workman. The impression is much increased by the quantities of leaves from the preceding year, which will generally be found on the earth beneath, for the horse-chestnut leaf is very durable, and retains its shape and substance long after it is dead and sapless. . . .

from *The Sylvan Year*
by PHILIP GILBERT HAMERTON (1834–1894)

THE chestnut splits its padded cell.
It opens an African eye.

A cabinet-maker, an old master
In the root of things, has done it again.

Its slippery gloss is a swoon,
A peek over the edge into—what?

Down the well-shaft of swirly grain,
Past the generous hands that lifted the May-lamps,

Into the Fairytale of a royal tree
That does not know about conkers

Or the war-games of boys.
Invisible though he is, this plump mare

Bears a tall armoured rider towards
The mirk-forest of rooty earth.

He rides to fight the North corner.
He must win a sunbeam princess

From the cloud castle of the rains.
If he fails, evil faces,

Jaws without eyes, will tear him to pieces.
If he succeeds, and has the luck

To snatch his crown from the dragon
Which resembles a slug

He will reign over our garden
For two hundred years.

from *Seasons Songs*
by TED HUGHES (1930–

91

Under a Wiltshire Apple Tree

Some folks as can afford,
So I've heard say,
Set up a sort of cross
Right in the garden way
To mind 'em of the Lord.

But I, when I do see
Thik apple tree
An' stoopin' limb
All spread wi' moss,
I think of Him
And how He talks wi' me.
I think of God.

And how He trod
That garden long ago;
He walked, I reckon, to and fro
And then sat down
Upon the groun'
Or some low limb
What suited Him,
Such as you see
On many a tree,
And on thik very one
Where I at set o' sun
Do sit and talk wi' He.

And, mornings, too, I rise and come
An' sit down where the branch be low;
A bird do sing, a bee do hum,
The flowers in the border blow,
And all my heart's so glad and clear
As pools be when the sun do peer,
As pools a-laughing in the light
When mornin' air is swep' an' bright,
As pools what got all Heaven in sight,
So's my heart's cheer
When he be near.

He never pushed the garden door,
He left no foot mark on the floor;
I never heard 'Un stir nor tread
And yet His hand do bless my head,
And when 'tis time for work to start
I takes Him with me in my heart.
And when I die, pray God I see
At very last thik apple tree
An' stoopin' limb,
And think of Him
And all He been to me.

ANNA DE BARY
written circa 1923

Mutability

THE sap is mounting back from that unseenness
darkly renewing in the common deep,
back to the light, and feeding the pure greenness
hiding in rinds round which the winds still weep.

The inner side of Nature is reviving,
another *sursum corda* will resound;
invisibly, a whole year's youth is striving
to climb those trees that look so iron-bound.

Preserving still that grey and cool expression,
the ancient walnut's filling with event;
while the young brush-wood trembles with repression
under the perching bird's presentiment.

RAINER MARIA RILKE (1875–1926)
trans. by J. B. Leishman

The Tree

OH, like a tree
Let me grow up to Thee!
  And like a tree
Send down my roots to Thee.

  Let my leaves stir
In each sigh of the air,
  My branches be
Lively and glad in Thee;

  Each leaf a prayer,
And green fire everywhere. . . .
  And all from Thee
The sap within the Tree.

  And let Thy rain
Fall – or as joy or pain,
  So that I be
Yet unforgot of Thee.

  Then shall I sing
The new song of Thy Spring,
  Every leaf of me
Whispering Love in Thee!

JOHN FREEMAN (1880–1929)

Autumn

THE leaves are falling, falling as from far,
as though above were withering farthest gardens;
they fall with a denying attitude.

And night by night, down into solitude,
the heavy earth falls far from every star.

We are all falling. This hand's falling too —
all have this falling-sickness none withstands.

And yet there's One whose gently-holding hands
this universal falling can't fall through.

RAINER MARIA RILKE (1875–1926)
trans. by J. B. Leishman

DREAMS or visions such as this, are, I fancy, of a kind that have not necessarily any significance. There are curlews of the imagination that suddenly go crying through waste spaces in the mind.

Of another, I think differently. "In the middle of a commonplace action of daily life suddenly I saw a woodland glade in twilight. A man lay before a fire, but when I looked closer I saw that what I thought was a fire was a mass of continually revolving leaves, though no leaf was blown from the maze, which was like an ever whirling yet never advancing wheel in the forest silence. He took up a reed-pipe or something of the kind. He played, and I saw the stars hang on the branches of the trees. He played, and I saw the great boles of the oaks become like amber filled with moonlight. He played, and then suddenly I realised that it was a still music, and had its life for me only in the symbol of colour. Flowers and plants and tree-growths of shape and hue such as I had never seen, and have never imagined, arose in the glade, which was now luminous as a vast shell behind which burned torches of honey-coloured flame.

"These changed continually as the red foliage of fire continually renewed itself. Then the player arose, and was a changing flame, and was gone. Another player was in the glade, where all was moveless shadow and old darkness. 'It is I, now, who am God', he said. Then he in turn was like a shadow of a reed in the wind, that a moment is, and is not. And I looked, and in the heart of the darkness saw a white light continually revolving: and in the silence was a voice. . . . 'And I – I am Life.'"

from *The Winged Destiny: Studies in the Spiritual History of the Gael*
by FIONA MacLEOD (William Sharp, 1856–1905)

RABBITS avoid close woodland, where the ground is shady, damp and grassless and they feel menaced by the undergrowth. Hazel did not care for the look of the trees. Still, he thought, Holly would no doubt think twice before following them into a place like that. . . .

From the moment he entered it the wood seemed full of noises. There was a smell of damp leaves and moss, and everywhere the splash of water went whispering about. Just inside, the brook made a little fall into a pool and the sound, enclosed among the trees, echoed as though in a cave. Roosting birds rustled overhead; the night breeze stirred the leaves; here and there a dead twig fell. And there were more sinister, unidentified sounds, from further away; sounds of movement.

from *Watership Down*
by RICHARD ADAMS (1920–

'What do you mean?' said Pippin. 'What is true?'

'The trees and the Ents,' said Treebeard. 'I do not understand all that goes on myself, so I cannot explain it to you. Some of us are still true Ents, and lively enough in our fashion, but many are growing sleepy, going tree-ish, as you might say. Most of the trees are just trees, of course, but many are half awake. Some are quite wide awake, and a few are, well, ah, well getting *Entish*. That is going on all the time.

'When that happens to a tree, you find that some have *bad* hearts. Nothing to do with their wood: I do not mean that. Why, I knew some good old willows down by the Entwash, gone long ago, alas! They were quite hollow, indeed they were falling all to pieces, but as quiet and sweet-spoken as a young leaf. And then there are some trees in the valleys under the mountains, sound as a bell, and bad right through. That sort of thing seems to spread. There used to be some very dangerous parts in this country. There are still some very black patches.'

'Like the Old Forest away to the north, do you mean?' asked Merry.

'Aye, aye, something like, but much worse. I do not doubt there is some shadow of the Great Darkness lying there still away north; and bad memories are handed down. But there are hollow dales in this land where the Darkness has never been lifted, and the trees are older than I am. Still, we do what we can. We keep off strangers and the foolhardy; and we train and we teach, we walk and we weed.

'We are tree-herds, we old Ents. Few enough of us are left now. Sheep get like shepherds, and shepherds like sheep, it is said; but slowly, and neither have long in the world. It is quicker and closer with trees and Ents, and they walk down the ages together. For Ents are more like Elves: less interested in themselves than Men are, and better at getting inside other things. And yet again Ents are more like Men, more changeable than Elves are, and quicker at taking the colour of the outside, you might say. Or better than both: for they are steadier and keep their minds on things longer.

'Some of my kin look just like trees now, and need something great to rouse them; and they speak only in whispers. But some of my trees are limb-lithe, and many can talk to me. Elves began it, of course, waking trees up and teaching them to speak and learning their tree-talk.'

from *The Lord of the Rings*
by J. R. R. TOLKIEN (1892–1973)

The Tree Uprooted

THE earth-bound giant now is free, is free;
    The last fight over, and the last moan still;
No tale of snow-clad heights where great dreams be,
    His exile heart can thrill.

Ah, how he cried with groaning branch and bough!
    For that far land beyond the sunshine morn,
For that lost joy tilled earth will not allow,
    That land where he was born.

Ah, how his heart that fought for freedom pined,
    His leaves, like restless fingers, tried to hold
The trailing garments of the passing wind,
    His struggle manifold.

The four winds heard and strove with mighty hands
    To bear him back to that far northern height
Where he was born; loosed from his earthly bands
    He poised, a moment's flight.

Then to the wind in passionate embrace
    His branches moved—out sung his parting breath.
He leaned to freedom from his prison place,
    Whose freedom was but death.

Better so lie, from this dire bondage free,
    O heart who knew the silence of the snows!
Than stand alone, O solitary tree,
    Where English greenwood grows.

Better to die than live in dull disgrace,
    O soul that dreamed the glory of the dream!
To be for sparrows but a resting place,
    Who heard the eagle scream.

DORA SIGERSON SHORTER (1872–1918)

ALL over the South-East yesterday, Britons were sawing
through sprawled tree trunks, patching up garden fences or
climbing through the scattered branches of once mighty trees.
At Sevenoaks, there was a distinct carnival atmosphere at the
local cricket ground, where, in Edwardian times, seven oaks
were planted. On Thursday, six of the seven were blown over
in a neat row. Yesterday children shrieked with delight as they
fought through the full-leafed branches on the ground.

article from *The Times*, 19 October 1987, on the great gales of
15 and 16 October

METHINKS I still hear, and am sure feel the dismal Groans (happening on the 26 Novemb. 1703) of our forests, so many thousands of goodly Oaks subverted by that late dreadful Hurricane; prostrating the Trees, and crushing all that grew under them, lying in ghastly Postures, like whole Regiments fallen in Battle, by the Sword of the Conqueror; Such was the Prospect for many Miles. . . . The losses and dreadful Stories of this Ruin were indeed great, but how much greater the Universal Devastation through the Kingdom! The Publick Account tells us, besides innumerable Men, reckoning no less than 3000 brave Oaks, in one part of the Forest of Dean blown down; and in New-Forest in Hampshire about 4000; and in about 450 Parks and Groves, from 200 large Trees to a 1000 of excellent Timber, without counting Fruit and Orchard Trees sans number. . . .

Sir Edward Harly had One thousand Three hundred blown down; My Self above 2000; several of which torn-up by their Fall, rais'd Mounds of Earth near 20 foot high, with great Stones intangled among the Roots and Rubbish; and this within almost sight of my Dwelling, sufficient to mortifie and change my too great Affection and Application to this Work; which, as I contentedly submit to, so I thank God, for what are yet left standing.

from *Sylva: A Discourse of Forest Trees*
(1706 edition) by JOHN EVELYN (1620–1706)

Ten O'Clock No More*

THE wind has thrown
The boldest of trees down.
Now disgraced it lies,
Naked in spring beneath the drifting skies,
Naked and still.

It was the wind
So furious and blind
That scourged half England through,
Ruining the fairest where most fair it grew
By dell and hill,

And springing here,
The black clouds dragging near,
Against this lonely elm
Thrust all his strength to maim and overwhelm
In one wild shock.

As in the deep
Satisfaction of dark sleep
The tree her dream dreamed on,
And woke to feel the wind's arms round her thrown
And her head rock.

And the wind raught
Her ageing boughs and caught
Her body fast again.
Then in one agony of age, grief, pain,
She fell and died.

Her noble height,
Branches that loved the light,
Her music and cool shade,
Her memories and all of her is dead
On the hill side.

But the wind stooped,
With madness tired, and drooped
In the soft valley and slept,
While morning strangely round the hush'd tree crept
And called in vain.

The birds fed where
The roots uptorn and bare
Thrust shameful at the sky;
And pewits round the tree would dip and cry
With the old pain.

'Ten o'clock's gone!'
Said sadly every one.
And mothers looking thought
Of sons and husbands far away that fought:—
And looked again.

*Ten o'clock is the name of a tall tree that crowned the eastern Cotswolds.

JOHN FREEMAN (1880–1929)

Willows

THEY pollard the willows
　　Until they look
Like the shaven head
　　Of a Dartmoor crook.

The willows are bald
　　As a water coot
Till all their branches
　　Begin to shoot;

Making a roof
　　For the country lane,
When somebody comes
　　And cuts them again.

REGINALD ARKNELL (1883–1959)

The Willow

LEANS now the fair willow, dreaming
Amid her locks of green.
In the driving snow she was parched and cold,
And in midnight hath been
Swept by blasts of the void night,
Lashed by the rains.
Now of that wintry dark and bleak
No memory remains.

In mute desire she sways softly;
Thrilling sap up-flows;
She praises God in her beauty and grace,
Whispers delight. And there flows
A delicate wind from the southern seas,
Kissing her leaves. She sighs.
While the birds in her tresses make merry;
Burns the Sun in the skies.

WALTER de la MARE (1873–1956)

THIS willow is as old to me as life;
And under it full often have I stretched,
Feeling the warm earth like a thing alive,
And gathering virtue in at every pore
Till it possessed me wholly, and thought ceased,
Or was transfused in something to which thought
Is coarse and dull of sense. Myself was lost,
Gone from me like an ache, and what remained
Became a part of the universal joy.
My soul went forth, and, mingling with the tree,
Danced in the leaves; or floating in the cloud,
Saw its white double in the stream below;
Or else, sublimed to pure ecstacy,
Dilated in the broad blue over all.

from *Under the Willows*
by JAMES RUSSELL LOWELL (1819–1891)

Trees

I THINK that I shall never see
A poem as lovely as a tree.

A tree whose hungry mouth is prest
Against the earth's sweet flowing breast;

A tree that looks at God all day,
And lifts her leafy arms to pray;

A tree that may in summer wear
A nest of robins in her hair;

Upon whose bosom snow has lain;
Who intimately lives with rain.

Poems are made by fools like me,
But only God can make a tree.

JOYCE KILMER (1888–1918)

Silver Birch

APRIL, she curtseys to the flying showers
In primaveral grace
Of nets and tassels, pennants, ribbons, gauzes,
Long tresses o'er her face.

July, through drench of sunlight, gloom of thunder,
In robe deep-water green,
Quiet she muses—only her birds break silence
Through leaves half-heard, half-seen.

With flame-bright veils she dares October music,
The wind's will her desire:
Sylvan Salome, swaying, tossing, glowing—
A ritual dance of fire.

Absolved of riot and colour, she meets December
With mien conventual, fine—
A pale Infanta in a proud black lace mantilla,
Austere and aquiline.

TERESA HOOLEY (pub. 1947)

The Rowan Tree

OH! Rowan Tree, Oh! Rowan Tree,
  thou'lt aye be dear to me;
Intwin'd thou art wi' mony ties o' hame
  and infancy.
Thy leaves were aye the first o' spring,
  Thy flow'rs the simmer's pride;
There was nae sic a bonny tree in a' the
  countrie side.
    Oh! Rowan Tree.

How fair wert thou in simmer time, wi' a'
  thy clusters white,
How rich and gay thy autumn dress, wi'
  berries red and bright!
On thy fair stem were mony names, which
  now nae mair I see,
But they're engraven on my heart—forgot
  they ne'er can be!
    Oh! Rowan Tree.

We sat aneath thy spreading shade, the
  bairnies round thee ran,
They pu'd thy bonny berries red, and
  necklaces they strang;
My mother! Oh! I see her still, she
  smiled our sports to see,
Wi' little Jeanie on her lap, an' Jamie at
  her knee!
    Oh! Rowan Tree.

Oh! there arose my father's prayer, in
  holy evening's calm,
How sweet was then my mother's voice,
  in the Martyr's psalm!
Now a' are gane! we meet nae mair
  aneath the Rowan Tree;
But hallowed thoughts around thee twine,
  o' hame and infancy.
    Oh! Rowan Tree.

BARONESS NAIRNE (1766–1845)
(Carolina Oliphant)

SUDDENLY the trees looked strangely beautiful:
'It has taken the form of trees,' I said,
'And I of a woman standing by a burn.'
So near I stood to your new state
I saw for a moment as you might
These sheltering boughs of spirit in its flight.
Shall you and I, in all the journeyings of soul,
Remember the rowan tree, the waterfall?

KATHLEEN RAINE (1908–

The Old Tree

THE wood shakes in the breeze
    Lifting its antlered heads;
Green leaf nor brown one sees
    But the rain's glassy beads.

One tree-trunk in the wood
    No tangled head uprears,
A stump of soft touchwood
    Dead to all hopes and fears.

Even the round-faced owl
    That shakes out his long hooting
With the moon cheek-a-jowl
    Could claw there no safe footing.

Riddled by worms' small shot,
    Empty of all desire,
It smoulders in its rot,
    A pillar of damp fire.

ANDREW YOUNG (1885–1971)

114

Dead Tree

LOOK, tower arboreal,
    unfortified by leaves,
    Surrender, Skeleton!
    Yet you persist, witch!
    The moon assumes
    you worship Her.
The crow still visits.
    You are the forest gallows
    Pulsing the underworld
    of worms.

ABEL STANION (1923–

FOR me, trees have always been the most penetrating preachers. I revere them when they live in tribes and families, in forests and groves. And even more I revere them when they stand alone. They are like lonely persons. Not like hermits who have stolen away out of some weakness, but like great, solitary men, like Beethoven and Nietzsche. In their highest boughs, the world rustles, their roots rest in infinity; but they do not lose themselves there, they struggle with all the force of their own laws, to build up their own form, to represent themselves. Nothing is holier, nothing is more exemplary than a beautiful, strong tree. When a tree is cut down and reveals its naked death-wound to the sun, one can read its whole history in the luminous, inscribed disk of its trunk: in the rings of its years, its scars, all the struggle, all the suffering, all the sickness, all the happiness and prosperity stand truly written, the narrow years and the luxurious years, the attacks withstood, the storms endured. And every young farmboy knows that the hardest and noblest wood has the narrowest rings, that high on the mountains and in continuing the most indestructible, the strongest, the ideal trees grow.

Trees are sanctuaries. Whoever knows how to speak to them, whoever knows how to listen to them, can learn the truth. They do not preach learning and precepts, they preach undeterred by particulars, the ancient law of life.

A tree says: A kernel is hidden in me, a spark, a thought, I am life from eternal life. The attempt and the risk that the eternal mother took with me is unique, unique the form and veins of my skin, unique the smallest play of leaves in my branches and the smallest scar on my bark. I was made to form and reveal the eternal in my smallest special detail.

A tree says: My strength is trust. I know nothing about my fathers. I know nothing about the thousand children that every year spring out of me. I live out the secret of my seed to the very end, and I care for nothing else. I trust that God is in me. I trust that my labor is holy. Out of this trust I live.

When we are stricken and cannot bear our lives any longer, then a tree has something to say to us: Be still! Be still! Look at me! Life is not easy, life is not difficult. Those are childish thoughts. Let God speak within you, and your thoughts will grow silent. You are anxious because your path leads away from mother and home. But every step and every day leads you back again to the mother. Home is neither here nor there. Home is within you, or home is nowhere at all.

A longing to wander tears my heart when I hear trees rustling in the wind at evening. If one listens to them silently for a long time, this longing reveals its kernel, its meaning. It is not so much a matter of escaping from one's suffering, though it may seem to be so. It is a longing for home, for a memory of the mother, for new metaphors for life. It leads home. Every path leads homeward, every step is birth, every step is death, every grave is mother.

(continued on page 118)

So the tree rustles in the evening, when we stand uneasy before out our childish thoughts. Trees have long thoughts, long-breathing and restful, just as they have longer lives than ours. They are wiser than we are, as long as we do not listen to them. But when we have learned how to listen to trees, then the brevity and the quickness and the childlike hastiness of our thoughts achieve an incomparable joy. Whoever has learned how to listen to trees no longer wants to be a tree. He wants to be nothing except what he is. That is home. That is happiness.

from *Wandering*
by HERMANN HESSE (1877–1962)

In the woods too, a man casts off his years, as the snake his slough, and at what period soever of life, is always a child. In the woods, is perpetual youth. Within these plantations of God, a decorum and sanctity reign, a perennial festival is dressed, and the guest sees not how he should tire of them in a thousand years. In the woods, we return to reason and faith. There I feel that nothing can befall me in life – no disgrace, no calamity (leaving me my eyes), which nature cannot repair. Standing on the bare ground – my head bathed by the blithe air, and uplifted into infinite space – all mean egotism vanishes. I become a transparent eye-ball; I am nothing; I see all; the currents of the Universal Being circulate through me; I am part or particle of God. . . . The greatest delight which the fields and woods minister, is the suggestion of an occult relation between man and the vegetable. They nod to me, and I do them. The waving of the boughs in the storm is new to me and old. It takes me by surprise, and yet is not unknown. Its effect is like that of a higher thought or a better emotion coming over me, when I deemed I was thinking justly or doing right.

from *Essays* (Nature)
by RALPH WALDO EMERSON (1803 –1882)

I REMEMBER, I remember,
The fir trees dark and high;
I used to think their slender tops
Were close against the sky:
It was a childish ignorance,
But now 'tis little joy
To know I'm further off from heav'n
Than when I was a boy.

from *I Remember, I Remember*
by THOMAS HOOD (1799 –1845)

My Cathedral

LIKE two cathedral towers these stately pines
    Uplift their fretted summits tipped with cones;
The arch beneath them is not built with stones,
    Not Art but Nature traced these lovely lines,
And carved this graceful arabesque of vines;
    No organ but the wind here sighs and moans,
No sepulchre conceals a martyr's bones,
    No marble bishop on his tomb reclines.
Enter! the pavement, carpeted with leaves
    Gives back a softened echo to thy tread!
Listen! the choir is singing; all the birds,
    In leafy galleries beneath the eaves,
Are singing! listen, ere the sound be fled,
    And learn there may be worship without words.

HENRY WADSWORTH LONGFELLOW (1807–1882)

WE had nearly threaded the wood, and were approaching an open grove of magnificent oaks on the other side, when sounds other than of nightingales burst on our ear, the deep and frequent strokes of the woodman's axe, and emerging from the Pinge we discovered the havoc which that axe had committed. Above twenty of the finest trees lay stretched on the velvet turf. There they lay in every shape and form of devastation: some, bare trunks stripped ready for the timber carriage, with the spoilers busy about them, stripping, hacking, hewing; others with their noble branches, their brown and fragrant shoots all fresh as if they were alive—majestic corpses, the slain of to-day! The grove was like a field of battle. The young lads who were stripping the bark, the very children who were picking up the chips, seemed awed and silent, as if conscious that death was around them. The nightingales sang faintly and interruptedly—a few low frightened notes like a requiem.

Ah! here we are at the very scene of murder, the very tree that they are felling; they have just hewn round the trunk with those slaughtering axes, and are about to saw it asunder. After all, it is a fine and thrilling operation, as the work of death usually is. Into how grand an attitude was that young man thrown as he gave the final strokes round the root; and how wonderful is the effect of that supple and apparently powerless saw, bending like a riband, and yet overmastering that giant of the woods, conquering and overthrowing that thing of life! Now it has passed half through the trunk, and the woodman has begun to calculate which way the tree will fall; he drives a wedge to direct its course;—now a few more movements of the noiseless saw; and then a larger wedge. See how the branches tremble! Hark how the trunk begins to crack! Another stroke of the huge hammer on the wedge, and the tree quivers, as with a mortal agony, shakes, reels, and falls. How slow, and solemn, and awful it is! How like to death, to human death in its grandest form! Caesar in the Capitol, Seneca in the bath, could not fall more sublimely than that oak.

from *Our Village*
by MARY RUSSELL MITFORD (1787–1855)

Roots are the branches down in the earth.
Branches are roots in the air.

———

Be still, my heart, these great trees are prayers.

———

RABINDRANATH TAGORE (1861–1941)
from *Stray Birds*

THE earthly manifestation of "God's world" began with the realm of plants, as a kind of direct communication from it. It was as though one were peering over the shoulder of the Creator, who, thinking himself unobserved, was making toys and decorations. Man and the proper animals, on the other hand, were bits of God that had become independent. That was why they could move about on their own and choose their abodes. Plants were bound for good or ill to their places. They expressed not only the beauty but also the thoughts of God's world, with no intent of their own and without deviation. Trees in particular were mysterious and seemed to me direct embodiments of the incomprehensible meaning of life. For that reason the woods were the place where I felt closest to its deepest meaning and to its awe-inspiring workings.

from *Memories, Dreams, Reflections*
by C. G. JUNG (1875–1961)

IN 'The Stones of Venice' Ruskin says "... Gradually as that monkish enthusiasm became more thoughtful, and as the sound of war became more and more intermittent beyond the gates of the convent or the keep, the stony pillars grew slender and the vaulted roof grew light, till they had wreathed themselves into the semblance of the summer woods at their fairest. . . ."

So that, after all, the solemn majesty of the forest aisles which we see translated into cold and silent stone in Gothic aisles, was, if not the source, the final inspiration. . . . In the beginning Man worshipped in groves, thence removed to temples with such architecture as the builders of his day provided. But we find that finally the church builders surrendered to the inspiration of Nature's original example, the over-arching grove – at once the most noble, the most solemn, the most godly of all enclosures known to man. The spirit of reverence is instinctively engendered by the subtle invitation of the arches; and the same Directive Force that shapes the wonderful flower and tree-forms in the ice on the window-panes, worked, apparently haphazard, in the temple arches towards the same arboreal articulation in stone.

from *English Woodlands and their Story*
by HOUGHTON TOWNLEY (pub. 1910)

The Worship of Trees

IN the religious history of the Aryan race in Europe the worship
of trees has played an important part. Nothing could be more
natural. For at the dawn of history Europe was covered with
immense primaeval forests, in which the scattered clearings
must have appeared like islets in an ocean of green. Down to
the first century before our era the Hercynian forest stretched
eastwards from the Rhine for a distance at once vast and
unknown; Germans whom Caesar questioned had travelled for
two months through it without reaching the end. Four
centuries later it was visited by the Emperor Julian, and the
solitude, the gloom, the silence of the forest appear to have
made a deep impression on his sensitive nature. He declared
that he knew nothing like it in the Roman empire. In our
country the wealds of Kent, Surrey, and Sussex are remnants
of the great forest of Anderida, which once clothed the whole
of the south-eastern portion of the island. Westwards it seems
to have stretched till it joined another forest that extended
from Hampshire to Devon. In the reign of Henry II the citizens
of London still hunted the wild bull and the boar in the woods
of Hampstead. Even under later Plantagenets the royal forests
were still sixty eight in number. In the forest of the Arden it
was said that down to modern times a squirrel might leap from
tree to tree for nearly the whole length of Warwickshire. . . .
From an examination of the Teutonic word for 'temple' Grimm
has made it probable that among the Germans the oldest
sanctuaries were natural woods. However that may be, tree-
worship is well attested for all the great European families of
the Aryan stock. Among the Celts the oak-worship of the
Druids is familiar to everyone, and their old words for
sanctuary seems to be identical in origin and meaning with the
Latin *nemus*, a grove or woodland glade, which still survives in
the name of Nemi. Sacred groves were common among the
ancient Germans, and tree-worship is hardly extinct among
their descendants at the present day. How serious that worship
was in former times may be gathered from the ferocious
penalty appointed by the old German laws for such as dared
to peel the bark of a standing tree. The culprit's navel was to
be cut out and nailed to the part of the tree till all his guts were
wound about its trunk. The intention of the punishment clearly
was to replace the dead bark by a living substitute taken from
the culprit; it was a life for a life, the life of a man for the life
of a tree.

from *The Golden Bough*
by J. G. FRAZER (1854 –1941)

IT seems that Donar, Thor's predecessor, like the Greek Zeus, was associated with the great oaks of the forest which covered much of Western Europe. The Germans, the Celts (whose thunder god was Tanaros), the Baltic tribes, and the Slavs all had holy groves within the forest where the thunder god was worshipped. Grimm suggested that the connection between the god and the oak was a practical one because the oak was the tree most often struck by lightning. The emphasis however, should probably be laid on the fact that when a great oak is struck by lightning, the sight of its destruction is something unforgettable. A vivid description of such a happening given by Tolstoy in *Anna Karenina* is worth quoting to illustrate this:

> '. . . Suddenly there was a glare of light, the whole earth seemed on fire, and the vault of heaven cracked overhead. Opening his blinded eyes, to his horror the first thing Levin saw through the thick curtain of rain between him and the woods was the uncannily altered position of the green crest of a familiar oak in the middle of the copse. 'Can it have been struck?' The thought had barely time to cross his mind when, gathering speed, the oak disappeared behind the other trees, and he heard the crash of the great tree falling on the others.'

There is little doubt that this is based on observation, and that Tolstoy had seen an oak falling in a storm. His impression that the heavens had opened and that fire from them was descending on to the earth is signinficant. As a channel through which the power of the sky god might reach down to the world of men, it is understandable that the mighty oak tree, itself a splendid symbol of age, strength, and endurance, came to be considered specially sacred to the Thunderer.

Groves which the Germans held sacred to the gods are mentioned by Tacitus at the end of the first century. Later on, a number of Christian missionaries – Boniface, Jerome, Bishop Otto, Willebrord – counted the felling of a tree sacred to a heathen god among their achievements in the cause of Christ.

from *Gods and Myths of Northern Europe*
by H. R. ELLIS DAVIDSON

AT the same time that we are earnest to explore and learn all things, we require that all things be mysterious and unexplorable, that land and sea be infinitely wild, unsurveyed, and unfathomed by us because unfathomable. We can never have enough of Nature. We must be refreshed by the sight of inexhaustible vigour, vast and Titanic features—the sea-coast with its wrecks, the wilderness with its living and its decaying trees, the thunder-cloud, and the rain which lasts three weeks and produces freshets. We need to witness our own limits transgressed, and some life pasturing freely where we never wander.

extract from *Walden* or *Life in the Woods*
by H. D. THOREAU (1817–1862)

AND so it is with all of us. Our lives, despite all the blows of fortune and misfortune, spring again and again from a mental root which we recognise as our real selves, which we want to express, which we must express, and to express which is our very life. But take a Tree, and you notice exactly the same thing. A dominant Idea informs the life of the Tree; persisting, it *forms* the tree. You may snip the leaves as much as you like to a certain pattern, but they will only grow in their own shape. You may cut off a branch, and another will take its place. You may remove a small twig, and even that twig will have within it the pervading character or purpose, for if you plant it in the ground, another tree of the same shape will spring from it. Finally you may cut the tree down root and branch, and burn it, but if there is left a single seed, within that seed in an almost invisible point lurks the formative ideal, which under proper conditions will again spring into life and expression. . . .

And now, at this time of year, there are lying and being buried in the great Earth thousands and thousands of millions of seeds of all kinds of plants and trees, which during the long winter will slumber there like little dream-images in the brain of the great globe, waiting for their awakening. And when the spring comes with the needful conditions, they will push forwards towards their expression and materialisation in the outer world, even as every thought presses towards its manifestation in us.

from *The Art of Creation*
by EDWARD CARPENTER (1844 –1929)

UPON hearing this Rata returned to his own village, and there reflected over many designs by which he might recover the bones of his father.

At length he thought of an excellent plan for this purpose, so he went into the forest and having found a very tall tree, quite straight throughout its entire length, he felled it, and cut off its noble branching top, intending to fashion the trunk into a canoe; and all the insects which inhabit trees, and the spirits of the forests, were very angry at this, and as soon as Rata had returned to the village at evening, when his day's work was ended, they all came and took the tree, and raised it up again, and the innumerable multitude of insects, birds, and spirits, who are called 'The offspring of Hakuturi', worked away at replacing each little chip and shaving in its proper place, and sang aloud their incantations as they worked; this was what they sang with a confused noise of various voices:

> Fly together, chips and savings,
> Stick ye fast together,
> Hold ye fast together;
> Stand upright again, O tree!

Early the next morning back came Rata, intending to work at hewing the trunk of his tree into a canoe. When he got to the place where he had left the trunk lying on the ground, at first he could not find it, and if that fine tall straight tree, which he saw standing whole and sound in the forest, was the same he thought he had cut down, there it was now erect again; however he stepped up to it, and manfully hewing away at it again, he felled it to the ground once more, and off he cut its fine branching top again, and began to hollow out the hold of the canoe, and to slope off its prow and the stern into their proper gracefully curved forms; and in the evening, when it became too dark to work, he returned to his village.

As soon as he was gone, back came the innumerable multitudes of insects, birds, and spirits, who are called the offspring of Hakuturi, and they raised up the tree upon its stump once more, and with a confused noise of various voices, they sang incantations as they worked, and when they had ended these, the tree again stood sound as ever in its former place in the forest.

The morning dawned, and Rata returned once more to work at his canoe. When he reached the place, was not he amazed to see the tree standing up in the forest, untouched, just as he had at first found it? But he, nothing daunted, hews way at it again, and down it topples crashing to the earth; as soon as he saw the tree upon the ground, Rata went off as if going home, and then turned back and hid himself in the underwood, in a spot whence he could peep out and see what took place; he had not been hidden long, when he heard the innumerable multitude of the children of Tane approaching the spot, singing their incantations as they came along; at last they arrived close to the place where the tree was lying upon the ground. Lo, a rush upon them is made by Rata. Ha, he has seized some of them; he shouts out to them, saying: 'Ha, ha, it is you, is it, then, who have been exercising your magical arts upon my tree?' Then the children of Tane all cried aloud in reply: 'Who gave you authority to fell the forest god to the ground? You had no right to do so.'

When Rata heard them say this, he was quite overcome with shame at what he had done.

from *Polynesian Mythology*
by SIR GEORGE GREY (1812–1892)

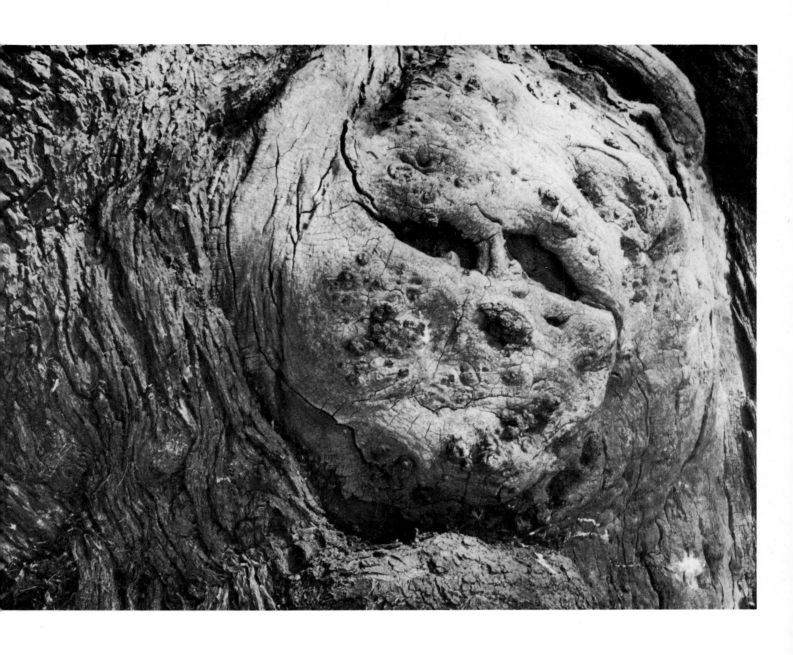

138

MAN that is born of woman is of few days and
                              full of trouble.
He cometh forth like a flower, and is cut down:
he fleeth also as a shadow, and continueth not.
And dost thou open thine eyes upon such an one,
and bringest me into judgement with thee?
Who can bring a clean thing out of an unclean?
                              not one.
Seeing his days are determined, the number of his
months are with thee, thou hast appointed his bounds
                              that he cannot pass;
Turn from him, that he may rest, till he shall
                              accomplish as an hireling, his day.
For there is hope of a tree, if it can be cut down, that
it will sprout again, and that the tender branch
                              thereof will not cease.
Though the root thereof wax old in the earth, and the
                              stock thereof die in the ground;
Yet through the scent of water it will bud, and bring
                              forth boughs like a plant.
But man dieth, and wasteth away: yea, man giveth up
                              the ghost, and where is he?

The Holy Bible: Job 14, v. 1–10
(Job's supplication to God for leniency)

The Aspen

MALISON be on thee, O aspen tree!
    On thee was crucified the King of the mountains,
In whom were driven the nails without clench,
    And that driving crucifying was exceeding sore –
    That driving crucifying was exceeding sore.

Malison be on thee, O aspen hard!
    On thee was crucified the King of glory,
Sacrifice of Truth, Lamb without blemish,
    His blood in streams down pouring –
    His blood in streams down pouring.

Malison be on thee, O aspen cursed!
    On thee was crucified the King of kings,
And malison be on the eye that seeth thee,
    If it maledict thee not, thou aspen cursed –
    If it maledict thee not, thou aspen cursed !

from *Carmina Gadelica (Incantations)*
by A. CARMICHAEL (pub. 1900).

IT is not growing like a tree
In bulk, doth make man better be;
Or standing long an oak, three hundred year,
To fall a log at last, dry, bald, and sere:
A lily of a day
Is fairer far in May,
Although it fall and die that night;
It was the plant and flower of light.
In small proportions we just beauties see;
And in short measures life may perfect be.

BEN JONSON (1573–1637)
from a poem in *Underwood*

Outlived by Trees

A BEECH, a cedar, and a lime
Grow on my lawn, embodying time.
A lime, a cedar, and a beech
The transience of this lifetime teach.
   Beech, cedar, lime, when I'm dead Me,
    You'll stand, lawn-shadowing, tree by tree;
    And in your greenery, while you last,
    I shall survive who shared your past.

SIEGFRIED SASSOON (1886–1967)

THERE is however, a deeper meaning in the sacred tree which Jung has developed at length in *Psychology of the Unconscious*. Fundamentally the tree of life is a mother image. Jung writes:

"Countless myths prove the derivation of man from trees; many myths show how the hero is enclosed in the maternal tree – thus dead Osiris in the column, Adonis in the myrtle, etc. Numerous female deities were worshipped as trees, from which resulted the cult of the sacred groves and trees. There is a transparent meaning in the legend where Attis castrates himself under a pine tree – i.e. it is because of the mother. Goddesses were often worshipped in the form of a tree or a piece of wood. Juno of Thespiae was a branch of a tree; Juno of Samos was a board; June of Argos, a column. The Carian Diana was an unworked piece of wood. Athene of Lindus was a polished column. . . . Tertullian calls an Attic Pallas *crucis stipes*, a wooden pole, or mast. The wooden pole is phallic, as the name suggests. . . ."

After giving many more examples Jung goes on:

"In this way we pass imperceptibly from the realm of mother-symbolism into the realm of male phallic symbolism. This element lies also in the tree, even in the family tree, as is distinctly shown in the medieval family tree. From the first ancestor the trunk of the great tree ascends in the place of the *membrum virile*. The bisexual symbolic character of the tree is intimated by the fact that in Latin trees have a masculine termination and a feminine gender."

from *The Mythology of the Soul*
by H. G. BAYNES (pub. 1940)

First, then, it shall be stated what correspondence is. The whole natural world corresponds to the spritual world, not only the natural world in general, but also in particular. Whatever, therefore, in the natural world exists from the spiritual, is said to be its correspondent. It must be understood that the natural world exists and subsists from the spiritual world, just as an effect exists from its efficient cause. By the natural world is meant whatever is under the sun and receives from it its heat and light; and all things which thence subsist belong to that world. But the spiritual world is heaven, and the things belonging to that world are all those which are in the heavens.

How the things of the vegetable kingdom correspond may appear from many considerations; as that little seeds grow into trees, which put forth leaves, produce flowers, and then fruit in which again they deposit seeds; and that these effects take place successively, and exist together in such admirable order, that it is impossible to describe them in a few words. Indeed, if volumes were written concerning them, still there would remain interior arcana, relating more closely to their uses, which could not be exhausted by science; and since these, also, are from the spiritual world, or heaven, which is in the form of man, as has been shown in a separate chapter, – therefore everything in this kingdom has a certain relation to something in man, as is known, also, to some in the learned world. That all things in this kingdom are correspondent, has been made evident to me by much experience. For very often when I have been in gardens, and have been looking at the trees, fruits, flowers, and vegetables, I have seen their correspondences in heaven, and have spoken with those in whom they were, and have been instructed concerning their origin and quality.

There is a similar correspondence with the things of the vegetable kingdom; thus a garden in general corresponds to heaven as to intelligence and wisdom; and on this account heaven is called the garden of God, and paradise, and by man, the heavenly paradise. Trees, according to their species, correspond to the perceptions and knowledges of good and truth, from which come intelligence and wisdom. On this account the ancients who were skilled in the knowledge of correspondences, held their sacred worship in groves. Hence also it is that trees are so often mentioned in the Word, and that heaven, the church, and man, are compared to the vine, the olive, the cedar, and other trees; and their good works to fruits. The food also derived from them, and especially from the harvest-seed from the field, corresponds to affections for good and truth; because these nourish spiritual life, as earthly food nourishes natural life.

from *Heaven and Hell*
by EMANUEL SWEDENBORG (1688–1772)

Elizabeth Wood

WAIL not, my *Wood*, thy Tree's untimely fall;
They were but Leaves that Autumn's blast could spoil.
The Bark bound up, and some fair Fruit withal,
Transplanted only, she exchanged her soil;
She is not dead, she did but fall to rise,
And leave the *Woods* to live in Paradise.

Epitaph in Low Leyton Church

IF all the seas were one sea,
What a *great* sea that would be!
And if all the trees were one tree,
What a *great* tree that would be!
And if all the axes were one axe,
What a *great* axe that would be!
And if all the men were one man,
What a *great* man that would be!
And if the *great* man took the *great* axe,
And cut down the *great* tree,
And let it fall into the *great* sea,
What a splish-splash that would be!

ANON.

Lament

WAE'S me, wae's me!
The acorn's not yet
Fallen from the tree
That's to grow the wood,
That's to make the cradle,
That's to rock the bairn,
That'll grow to the man
Who's to lay me!

ANON.

AND do you remember what secrets the trees told us as we lay
under their shady branches on the hot midsummer days, while
the leaves danced and flickered against the blue, blue sky? Can
you tell what was the charm that held us like a dream in the
falling dusk as we watched their heavy masses grow dark and
gloomy against the silvery twilight sky? . . .

from *Trees Shown to the Children*
by J. H. KELMAN and C. E. SMITH (pub. 1908)

Wood Grain

THIS is the way that the sap-river ran
From the root to the top of the tree
   Silent and dark
   Under the bark
Working a wonderful plan
   That the leaves never know
   And the branches that grow
On the brink of the tide, never see.

JOHN BANNISTER TABB (1845–1909)

Green

"I DID not think",
said she with a frown,
"Tree trunks are green
and not just brown.

Until today if you
had asked me,
I would have said
(and said quite crossly),

Trunks are brown and
LEAVES are green".

"Have you never really seen –
Until just now, what
colours abound?
Open your eyes child
and look around.

See what you see,
not what you know.

We have a long, long, way to go . . ."

ANNE DUNFORD (1946–

WOOD is necessary to civilised life, and therefore it is a basis of civilisation. But wood may be regarded as merely a by-product of trees. Their greatest value is probably their beneficient effect upon life, health, climate, soil, rainfall and streams. Trees beautify the country, provide shade for humans and stock, shelter crops from wind and storm and retain the water in the soil at a level at which it can be used by man. The neglect of forestry in the past has accounted for the deserts that exist, because of the fact that when the tree covering disappears from the earth, the water-level sinks.

A man can live less than five weeks without food, and trees make the production of food possible by improving the quality of soil, supplying cereals, fruit, honey, sugar and nuts, giving moisture and making grazing land for cattle.

We live less than five days without air, and trees purify the air by absorbing carbon dioxide exhaled by man, and throw out the pure oxygen, so necessary to life.

In short, the quantity of our food, the purity of water and air depend upon trees.

Trees then, are not such a 'wooden' subject as they may at first appear to be. At any rate they deserve our consideration, for our attitude towards them to-day may determine the feast or famine of to-morrow. Their presence or absence may decide for posterity health or disease, food or starvation, pure water, or rectified fluids, crops or failure, rain or floods, helpful birds or harmful insects, prosperity or poverty, pure air or foul air, fertile or desert land – we may have our choice. When the forests go, the waters go, the fish and game go, crops go, herds and flocks go, fertility departs. The age-old phantoms appear, stealthily, one after another – Flood, Drought, Fire, Famine, Pestilence.

from *I Planted Trees*
by RICHARD ST BARBE BAKER (1889–1982)
(founder of the Society 'The Men of the Trees').

Nay, nay, Ivy,
It may not be, I wis,
For Holly must have the mastry
As the maner is.

HOLLY bereth beris,
Beris rede enough;
The thristilcok, the popingay
Daunce in every bough.
Welaway, sory Ivy!
What fowlès hast thou,
But the sory howlet
That singeth 'How how'?

Nay, nay, Ivy. . . .

Ivy bereth beris
As blak as any sloe.
There commeth the woode colver,
And fedeth her of tho;
She lifteth up her taill
And she cakkès or she go;
She wold not for an hundred pound
Serve Holly so.

Nay, nay, Ivy. . . .

Holly with his mery men
They can daunce in hall;
Ivy and her jentell women
Can not daunce at all,
But like a meine of bullokès
In a water fall,
Or on a hot somers day
Whan they be mad all.

Nay, nay, Ivy. . . .

Holly and his mery men
Sitt in cheires of gold;
Ivy and her jentell women
Sitt without in fold,
With a paire of kibèd
Helès caught with cold.
So wold I that every man had
That with Ivy will hold!

Nay, nay, Ivy,
It may not be, I wis,
For Holly must have the mastry
As the maner is.

ANONYMOUS (15th C.)

howlet = owl
colver = pigeon
tho = them
meine = company
kibèd = chilblains
helès = heels

150

151

The Babes in the Wood

MY dear, do you know,
How a long time ago,
    Two poor little children,
Whose names I don't know,
Were stolen away
On a fine summer's day,
    And left in a wood,
As I've heard people say.

Among the trees high
Beneath the blue sky
    They plucked the bright flowers
And watched the birds fly;
Then on blackberries fed,
And strawberries red,
    And when they were weary
'We'll go home,' they said.

And when it was night
So sad was their plight,
    The sun it went down,
And the moon gave no light.
They sobbed and they sighed
And they bitterly cried,
    And long before morning
They lay down and died.

And when they were dead,
The robins so red
    Brought strawberry leaves
And over them spread;
And all the day long,
The green branches among,
    They'd prettily whistle
And this was their song—
'Poor babes in the wood!
Sweet babes in the wood!
    Oh the sad fate of
The babes in the wood!'

ANONYMOUS (c. 1800)

To the Oaks of Glencree

MY arms are round you, and I lean
Against you, while the lark
Sings over us, and golden lights, and green
Shadows are on your bark.

There'll come a season when you'll stretch
Black boards to cover me:
Then in Mount Jerome I will lie, poor wretch,
With worms eternally.

J. M. SYNGE (1871–1909)

The Magic Wood

THE wood is full of shining eyes,
The wood is full of creeping feet,
The wood is full of tiny cries:
You must not go to the wood at night!

I met a man with eyes of glass
And a finger as curled as the wriggling worm,
And hair all red with rotting leaves,
And a stick that hissed like a summer snake.

He sang me a song in backwards words,
And drew me a dragon in the air.
I saw his teeth through the back of his head,
And a rat's eyes winking from his hair.

He made me a penny out of stone,
And showed me the way to catch a lark
With a straw and a nut and a whispered word
And a pennorth of ginger wrapped up in a leaf.

He asked me my name, and where I lived;
I told him a name from my Book of Tales;
He asked me to come with him into the wood
And dance with the Kings from under the hills.

But I saw that his eyes were turning to fire;
I watched the nails grow on his wriggling hand;
And I said my prayers, all out in a rush,
And found myself safe on my father's land.

Oh, the wood is full of shining eyes,
The wood is full of creeping feet,
The wood is full of tiny cries:
You must not go to the wood at night!

HENRY TREECE (1912–1967)

Faust:

How the wind-hag races through the air!
How she slaps my shoulder with her blast.

Mephistopheles:

You must grasp these ancient ribs of rock,
or else she'll hurl you down headlong.
The mist is thickening the night.
Hear the timbers creak and moan;
frightened owls are streaking through the trees.
Hear through the palaces of evergreen
the towering pillars crack and shatter,
the squeal and crash of tumbling branches!
The hollow thunder of the trunks!
The yawning of the roots below!
With a furious roar and rumble
they fall into a tangled heap. . . .

from *Faust (Walpurgis Night)*
by J. W. VON GOETHE (1749 –1832)

BRANCH-RUNES learn, if a healer wouldst be,
And cure for wounds would work;
On the bark thou shalt write, and on trees that be
With boughs to the eastward bent.

from the German story of *Sigund*
and *Brynhild* (c. 9th C.)

158

THERE is a Yew-tree, pride of Lorton Vale,
Which to this day stands single, in the midst
Of its own darkness, as it stood of yore:
Not loth to furnish weapons for the bands
Of Umfraville or Percy ere they marched
To Scotland's heaths; or those that crossed the sea
And drew their sounding bows at Azincour,
Perhaps at earlier Crecy, or Poitiers.
Of vast circumference and gloom profound
This solitary Tree! a living thing
Produced too slowly ever to decay;
Of form and aspect too magnificent
To be destroyed. But worthier still of note
Are those fraternal Four of Borrowdale,
Joined in one solemn and capacious grove;
Huge trunks! and each particular trunk a growth
Of untwisted fibres serpentine
Up-coiling, and inveterately convolved;
Nor uninformed with Phantasy, and looks
That threaten the profane; – a pillared shade,
Upon whose grassless floor of red-brown hue,
By sheddings from the pining umbrage tinged
Perennially – beneath whose sable roof
Of boughs, as of for festal purpose, decked
With unrejoicing berries – ghostly shapes
May meet at noontide; Fear and trembling Hope,
Silence and Foresight; Death the Skeleton
And Time the Shadow; – there to celebrate,
As in a natural temple scattered o'er
With altars undisturbed of mossy stone,
United worship; or in mute repose
To lie, and listen to the mountain flood
Murmuring from Glaramara's inmost caves.

WILLIAM WORDSWORTH (1770– 1850)

AND so this man returned with axe and saw
At evening close from killing the tall treen,
The soul of whom by Nature's gentle law

Was each a wood-nymph, and kept ever green
The pavement and the roof of the wild copse,
Chequering the sunlight of the blue serene

With jaggèd leaves, – and from the forest tops
Singing the winds to sleep – or weeping oft
Fast showers of aëreal water-drops

Into their mother's bosom, sweet and soft,
Nature's pure tears which have no bitterness; –
Around the cradles of the birds aloft

They spread themselves into the loveliness
Of fan-like leaves, and over pallid flowers
Hang like moist clouds: – or, where high branches kiss,

Make a green space among the silent bowers,
Like vast fane in a metropolis,
Surrounded by the columns and the towers

All overwrought with branch-like traceries
In which there is religion – and the mute
Persuasion of unkindled melodies,

Odours and gleams and murmurs, which the lute
Of the blind pilot-spirit of the blast
Stirs as it sails, now grave and now acute,

Wakening the leaves and waves, ere it has passed
To such brief unison as on the brain
One tone, which never can recur, has cast,
One accent never to return again.

. . . .

The world is full of Woodmen who expel
Love's gentle Dryads from the haunts of life,
And vex the nightingales in every dell.

The Woodman and the Nightingale (second part)
by PERCY BYSSHE SHELLEY (1792–1822)

160

Frosted Trees

OH, what a goodly and glorious show!
  The stately trees have decked themselves with white,
  And stand transfigured in a robe of light;
Wearing for each lost leaf a flake of snow.
The rising sun shines through them with a glow
  Of gold amid the silver; while a bright
  But hapless bird comes hovering into sight,
Amazed at the wan world above, below.

What was the ivory house which Ahab made
  Compared with Nature's fretwork rich and rare,
In every grove with lavish wealth displayed?
  And oh, if frozen mist appears so fair,
How will those "many mansions" be arrayed,
  Which Love is fashioning in celestial air!

RICHARD WILTON (1827–1903)

162

HOWEVER, without doubt the largest single reason for the loss of trees is Dutch Elm Disease. So far, over half the elms (12 million) in the southern half of the country have died and the rest appear doomed to follow.

from a BBC booklet *British Trees*
from the series *Crisis in the Countryside* 1978

IT is caused by a fungus which produces a toxic matter and causes the blocking of the sap-conducting cells with a gum-like substance. . . . The fungus is intimately connected with and spread by the large and small elm bark beetles. These creatures breed in galleries that they mine under the bark of elm-trees, and it is in these galleries that the fungus fructifies. The young beetles that emerge carry the spores with them, which they deposit in the young shoots of healthy trees upon which they feed.

from *British Trees (A Guide for Everyman)*
by MILES HADFIELD (pub. 1957)

The Shepherd's Tree

HUGE elm, with rifted trunk all notched and scarred,
    Like to a warrior's destiny, I love
To stretch me often on thy shadowed sward,
    And hear the laugh of summer leaves above;
Or on thy buttressed roots to sit, and lean
    In careless attitude, and there reflect
On times and deeds and darings that have been—
    Old castaways, now swallowed in neglect,
While thou art towering in thy strength of heart,
    Stirring the soul to vain imaginings
In which life's sordid being hath no part.
    The wind of that eternal ditty sings
Humming of future things, that burn the mind
To leave some fragment of itself behind.

JOHN CLARE (1793–1864)

The Holly Tree

O READER! hast thou ever stood to see
 The holly tree?
The eye that contemplates it well perceives
 Its glossy leaves
Order'd by an intelligence so wise,
As might confound the Atheist's sophistries.

Below a circling fence, its leaves are seen
 Wrinkled and keen;
No grazing cattle through their prickly round
 Can reach to wound;
But as they grow where nothing is to fear,
Smooth and unarm'd the pointless leaves appear.

I love to view these things with curious eyes,
 And moralize:
And in this wisdom of the holly tree
 Can emblems see
Wherewith perchance to make a pleasant rhyme,
One which may profit in the after-time.

Thus, though abroad perchance I might appear
 Harsh and austere,
To those who on my leisure would intrude
 Reserved and rude,
Gentle at home amid my friends I'd be,
Like the high leaves upon the holly tree.

And should my youth, as youth is apt, I know
 Some harshness show,
All vain asperities I day by day
 Would wear away,
Till the smooth temper of my age should be
Like the high leaves upon the holly tree.

And as when all the summer trees are seen
 So bright and green,
The holly leaves their fadeless hues display
 Less bright than they;
But when the bare and wintry woods we see
What then so cheerful as the holly tree?

So serious should my youth appear among
 The thoughtless throng,
So would I seem amid the young and gay
 More grave than they,
That in my age as cheerful I might be
As the green winter of the holly tree.

ROBERT SOUTHEY (1774 –1843)

THERE are some men, of course, some men, I know,
Who, when they pass,
Seem like trees walking, and to grow
From earth, and, native in the grass,
(So taut their muscles) move on gliding roots.
They blossom every day; their fruits
Are always new and cover the happy ground.
Wherever they may stand
You hear inevitable sound
Of birds and branches, harvest and all delights
Of pastured and wooded land.
For them it is not dangerous to go
Each side that barrier moving to and fro:
They without trepidation moderate
Excursions into sleep, and safely come awake.

But it is different, different for me,
(Also for you I fear)
To whom a tree seems something more than tree,
And when we see,
Clustered together, two or three,
We almost are afraid to pass them near.
How beautifully they grow,
Above their stiles and lanes and watery places,
Crowding the brink of silence everywhere,
With branches dipping low
To smile toward us or to stroke our faces.
They drown us in their summer, and swirl round,
Leaving us faint: so nobody is free,
But always some surrounding ground
Is swamped and washed and covered in by tree.

They follow us and haunt us. We must build
Houses of wood. Our evening rooms are filled
With fragments of the forest: chairs and tables.
We swing our wooden doors;
Pile up, divide our sheds, byres, stables
With logs, make wooden stairs, lay wooden floors,
Sit, move, and sleep among the limbs of trees,
Rejoicing to be near them. How men saw,
Chisel and hammer, carve and tease
All timber to their purpose, modelling
The forest in their chambers. And the raw
Wild stuff, build like a cupboard or a shelf,
Will crack and shiver in the night, and sing,
Reminding everybody of itself;
Out of decayed old centuries will bring
A sudden memory
Of growing tree.

from *Trees*
by HAROLD MONRO (1879–1932)

The Beech Tree's Petition

O LEAVE this barren spot to me!
Spare, woodman, spare the beechen tree!
Though bush or flower never grow
My dark unwarming shade below;
Nor summer bud perfume the dew
Of rosy blush, or yellow hue;
Nor fruits of autumn, blossom-born,
My green and glossy leaves adorn;
Nor murmuring tribes from me derive
Th' ambrosial amber of the hive;
Yet leave this barren spot to me:
Spare woodman, spare the beechen tree!

Thrice twenty summers I have seen
The sky grow bright, the forest green;
And many a wintry wind have stood
In bloomless, fruitless solitude,
Since childhood in my pleasant bower
First spent its sweet and sportive hour;
Since youthful lovers in my shade
Their vows of truth and rapture made,
And on my trunk's surviving frame
Carved many a long-forgotten name.
Oh! by the sighs of gentle sound,
First breathed upon this sacred ground;
By all that love has whisper'd here,
Or Beauty heard with ravish'd ear;
As Love's own altar honour me:
Spare, woodman, spare the beechen tree.

THOMAS CAMPBELL (1777–1844)

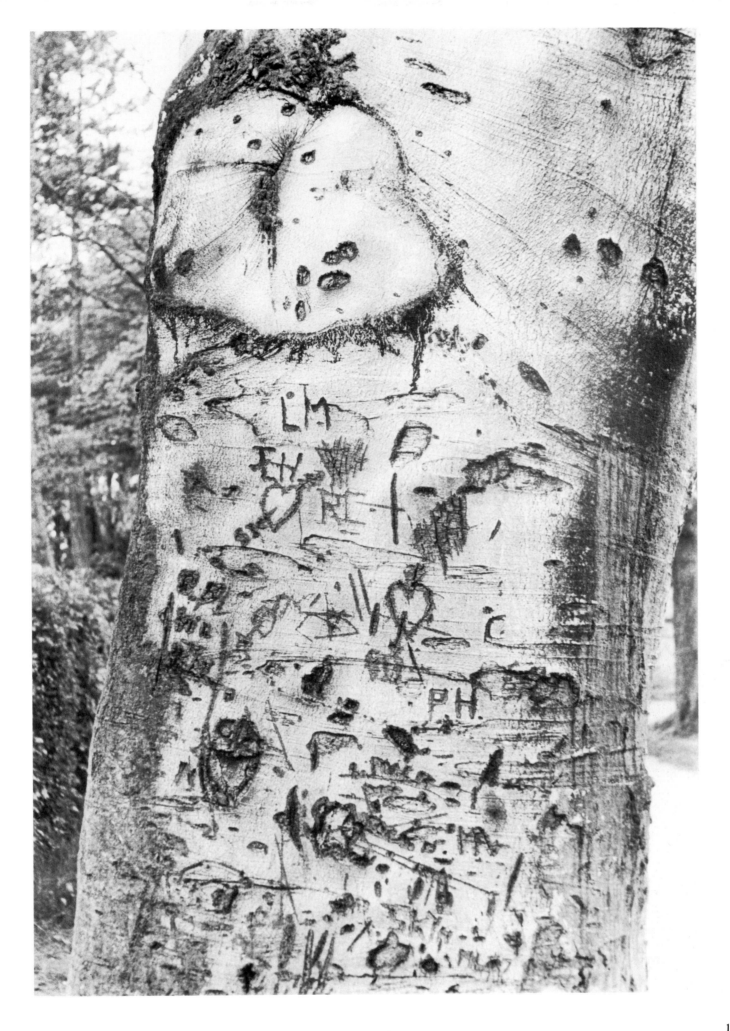

Binsey Poplars
felled 1879

My aspens dear, whose airy cages quelled,
Quelled or quenched in leaves the leaping sun,
All felled, felled, are all felled;
  Of a fresh and following folded rank
      Not spared, not one
        That dandled a sandalled
     Shadow that swam or sank
On meadow and river and wind-wandering weed-winding
  bank.

  O if we but knew what we do
     When we delve or hew –
   Hack and rack the growing green!
      Since country is so tender
   To touch, her being só slender,
   That, like this sleek and seeing ball
   But a prick will make no eye at all,
   Where we, even where we mean
      To mend her we end her,
   When we hew or delve:
After-comers cannot guess the beauty been.
  Ten or twelve, only ten or twelve
   Strokes of havoc únselve
    The sweet especial scene,
   Rural scene, a rural scene,
   Sweet especial rural scene.

GERARD MANLEY HOPKINS (1844 –1889)

EVERY one has heard the story which has gone the rounds of New England, of a strong and beautiful bug which came out of the dry leaf of an old table of apple-tree wood, which had stood in a farmer's kitchen for sixty years, first in Connecticut, and afterward in Massachusetts, – from an egg deposited in the living tree many years earlier still, as appeared by counting the annual layers beyond it; which was heard gnawing out for several weeks, hatched perchance by the heat of an urn. Who does not feel his faith in a resurrection and immortality strengthened by hearing of this? Who knows what beautiful and winged life, whose egg has been buried for ages under many concentric layers of woodenness in the dead dry life of society, deposited at first in the alburnum of the green and living tree, which has been gradually converted into the semblance of its well-seasoned tomb, – heard perchance gnawing out now for years by the astonished family of man, as they sat round the festive board, – may unexpectedly come forth from amidst society's most trivial and handselled furniture, to enjoy its perfect summer life at last!

extract from *Walden* or *Life in the Woods*
by H. D. THOREAU (1817–1862)

THE man who loves trees is fortunate, for by an immutable law of Nature, in return for his love, he is able to gather an indefinable sense of exhilaration and power and share a portion of the attributes of the object of his love. Trees are for ever giving out an element which is healthful and exhilarating, and is it too much to believe that a tree responds in proportion to the love that is given to it? Among foresters and nurserymen it has often been observed that some get more response than others from the trees of their planting; they grow for them better than for others. To all outward appearances, the same cultivation is given, but the response is different.

To my way of thinking, it is that the tree responds to or shows its pleasure in return for loving care. There are some people who might ridicule the idea of a tree thinking, but let me remind them that a tree has an organised body of depending parts, fulfilling functions necessary to the life of the tree. Its organism is akin to our own in many respects. It has for blood, its sap. It has a circulatory system. It has for skin, bark. It has for lungs, its leaves. Like ourselves, it must have food, and the tree draws its nourishment from the soil and air and sunlight.

The tree adapts itself to circumstances. Sir Jagadis Bose, as also the Austrian forestry research students, have proved that the tree has heart beats and that the pulsatory reactions of a plant are exactly parallel to those of a human being or animal. It responds to stimulants and can be put to sleep under an anaesthetic. Its growth can be arrested or stimulated by electricity and it can feel an electric shock. A sensitive plant such as the *Mimosa pudica* recoils at the touch of a man's hand, transmitting shock effects along different nervous channels or, when growing in the wild, it escapes danger from grazing cattle, for with a touch of their foot it becomes invisible to them, sinking down in the grass until threat of damage is past.

from *I Planted Trees*
by RICHARD ST BARBE BAKER (1889–1982)

WE began amongst trees. Can we imagine now what it was like living in the days of that beginning? We can have some idea; for though the corrosions of Time do carve incredible changes on the creatures and the landscapes of the earth, there are some things which repeat themselves so closely as seeming to ignore the passage of centuries. Amongst such we may consider the tropical forests of today. If we know something of them we can imagine something of the environment of our earliest ancestors, and therefore something of their feelings. They came into the first glimmerings of consciousness in the forests. That was their world, all they saw, all they knew – a world of trees. . . .

from *The Vision of Glory*
by JOHN STEWART COLLIS (1900–1984)

THOUSANDS of books that have given rapturous delight to
millions of ingenious minds for Wordsworth were absolutely
a dead letter – closed and sealed up from his sensibilities and
his powers of appreciation, not less than colours from a blind
man's eye. Even the few books which his peculiar mind had
made indispensible to him were not in such a sense
indispensible as they would have been to a man of more
sedentary habits. He lived in the open air, and the enormity of
pleasure which both he and his sister drew from the common
appearances of nature and their everlasting variety – variety so
infinite that, if no one leaf of a tree or shrub ever exactly
resembled another in all its filaments and their arrangement,
still less did any one day ever repeat another in all its
pleasurable elements. This pleasure was to him in the stead of
many libraries: –

> "One impulse, from a vernal wood,
>   Could teach him more of Man,
> Of moral evil and of good,
>   Than all the sages can."

from *Reminiscences of the English Lake Poets*
by THOMAS DE QUINCEY (1785–1859)

MAN should enter the woods, not with any conquistador obsession or mighty hunter complex, neither in a spirit of braggadocio, but rather with the awe, and not a little of the veneration, of one who steps within the portals of some vast and ancient edifice of wondrous architecture. For many a man who considers himself the master of all he surveys would do well, when setting foot in the forest, to take off not only his hat but his shoes too, and in not a few cases, be glad he is allowed to remain in an erect position. And he might come to it, at that; for the woods, in time, sometimes a very short time, will make either a man or a monkey of you.

from *Tales of an Empty Cabin*
by GREY OWL (Archibald Stansfield Belaney, 1888–1938)

176

In a Wood

PALE beech and pine-tree blue,
   Set in one clay,
Bough to bough cannot you
   Bide out your day?
When the rains skim and skip,
Why mar sweet comradeship,
Blighting with poison-drip
   Neighbourly spray?

Heart-halt and spirit-lame,
   City-oprest,
Unto this wood I came
   As to a nest;
Dreaming that sylvan peace
Offered the harrowed ease –
Nature a soft release
   From men's unrest.

But, having entered in,
   Great growths and small
Show them to men akin –
   Combatants all!
Sycamore shoulders oak,
Bines the slim sapling yoke,
Ivy-spun halters choke
   Elms stout and tall.

Touches from ash, O wych,
   Sting you like scorn!
Yóu, too, brave hollies, twitch
   Sidelong from thorn.
Even the rank poplars bear
Illy a rival's air,
Cankering in blank despair
   If overborne.

Since, then, no grace I find
   Taught me of trees
Turn I back to my kind,
   Worthy as these.
There at least smiles abound,
There discourse trills around,
There, now and then, are found
   Life-loyalties.

from *Wessex Poems*
by THOMAS HARDY (1840–1928)

THE rule is that the more delicate and beautiful the flower and fruit the closer must be the union with earth. And the point of contact is the root. There colour and scent are made; there the hundred-foot tree lies in little; there the petal that a dewdrop almost destroys is held safe under the ponderous earth. In the root, when April comes, Someone awakes, rubs drowsy eyes, stretches drowsy hands, remembers a dream of light that troubled its sleep, and begins, with infinite precautions, finesse and courage, to work the miracle of which it has knowledge; 'eagerly watching for its flower and fruit, anxious its little soul looks out.'

Surely no idea of God could so well hint of Him as the idea of the root – of the great root of a forest tree, hawsered in the heart of matter; upholding matter; transforming matter by a secret alchemy into beauty that goes out from mystery – lives its day – returns, weary, into mystery, and is again renewed.

'None can tell how from so small a centre come such sweets.'

from *Spring of Joy*
by MARY WEBB (1881–1927)

THUS, the dead leaf, fallen wood, the fruit casings and fallen petals, the frass bored and churned by a billion billion wood-boring beetles, the corpses of animals, everything that has been born, has lived and died, is treated according to its nature in that vast factory where the roots of countless plants ceaselessly seek moisture-borne food to maintain and increase the woody stems of trees coveted by man.

The air, breathed in by leaf and root alike, supplies not only the oxygen vital to plants and animals, but the gas carbon dioxide. This by some unknown alchemy is bisected, the carbon being retained to make sugars and starches. The oxygen is released into the atmosphere.

The most common component of the air, nitrogen, comprising more than three-quarters of its bulk, though essential to life, can not directly be utilized by the plant. Nitrogen is needed for the production of tissue-building proteins, the foundation of protoplasm, and of all life. The soil provides some nitrogen by the continued break-down of decaying organic material and from the slowly decaying rocks. But not enough.

In the soil the minute threads of fungi are sometimes capable of 'fixing' gaseous nitrogen and turning it into usable nitrates. But the chief fixers of nitrogen are certain bacteria which achieve what the plants themselves cannot. These soil dwellers absorb the gas nitrogen from the soil air, and by an obscure chemistry produce soluble forms of nitrogen capable of being absorbed by all plants. Some of these bacteria live a free existence; others live in close association with certain plants, forming small nodules attached to the roots.

Within these nodules, which are just visible to the naked eye, is the plant's own liquid food; in return they provide nitrogen in assimilable form.

The plants of the forest wage a constant struggle among themselves; an unceasing battle for light and food, but a battle without visible strife, or noise, or discernible movement, but nevertheless a battle that is fierce and unabating. Day and night plants grapple constantly with the problems of water and light.

from *The Perpetual Forest*
by W. V. COLLINS (pub. 1958)

CARE is taken that trees do not grow into the sky.

J. W. VON GOETHE (1749–1832)

The Wych-Elm

IN weariness of heart,
Bitter with false labour,
I put the world apart
And seek an old neighbour.

A century or more
He has mused and murmured
Over my door
Of what the winds rumoured.

I am never tired
Of his leaf-lippings,
Garrulous, absurd
In his bough-whippings.

He will rub his branches
Like a musing fly,
Though his great haunches
Are three cottages high.

He will squeak in the night
Like a foraging mouse,
And tremble with fright
Above the house.

He will affront the moon
With antics of folly,
And next day at noon
Sham green melancholy.

As I say to the woman
Who shares my cottage,
"The tree's almost human
In its whimsical dotage!"

RICHARD CHURCH (1893–1972)

The Elms

FINE as the dust of plumy fountains blowing
Across the lanterns of a revelling night,
The tiny leaves of April's earliest growing
Powder the trees – so vapourously light,
They seem to float, billows of emerald foam
Blown by the South on its bright airy tide,
Seeming less trees than things beatified,
Come from the world of thought which was their home.

For a while only. Rooted strong and fast,
Soon will they lift towards the summer sky
Their mountain-mass of clotted greenery.
Their immaterial season quickly past,
They grow opaque, and therefore needs must die,
Since every earth to earth returns at last.

ALDOUS HUXLEY (1894–1963)

THE stagnant water in the hollow trees [beech] cures the most obstinate tetters, scabs, and scurfs in man or beast, fomenting the part with it. The leaves chewed are wholesome for the gums and teeth; and the very buds, as they are in winter hardened and dried upon the twigs make good tooth-pickers. Swine may be driven to mast about the end of August; but it is observed, that, when they feed upon it before it is mature, it intoxicates them for a while; and that, generally, their fat is not so good and solid, but drips away too soon. In the meantime the kernels of the mast are greedily devoured by squirrels, mice, and, above all, by doormice, who, harbouring in the hollow trees, grow so fat, that, in some countries abroad, they take infinite numbers of them, I suppose, to eat. And what relief they give to thrushes, black-birds, fieldfares, and other birds, everybody knows.

from *Sylva: A Discourse of Forest Trees*
by JOHN EVELYN (1620 –1706)

THE feeling, however, was evoked more powerfully by trees than by even the most supernatural of my flowers; it varied in power according to time and place and the appearance of the tree or trees, and always affected me most on moonlight nights. Frequently, after I had first begun to experience it consciously, I would go out of my way to meet it, and I used to steal out of the house alone when the moon was at its full to stand, silent and motionless, near some group of large trees, silvered by the beams; and at such times the sense of mystery would grow until a sensation of delight would change to fear, and the fear increase until it was no longer to be borne, and I would hastily escape to recover the sense of reality and safety indoors, where there was light and company. . . .

. . . I imagine it would be correct to describe the sensation experienced on those moonlight nights among the trees as similar to the feeling a person would have if visited by a supernatural being, if he was perfectly convinced that it was there in his presence, albeit silent and unseen, intently regarding him, and divining every thought in his mind.

from *Far Away and Long Ago*
by W. H. HUDSON (1841–1922)

SHE continually peeped out through the lattice, but could see little. In front lay the brown leaves of last year, and upon them some yellowish green ones of this season that had been prematurely blown down by the gale. Above stretched an old beech, with vast arm-pits, and great pocket-holes in the sides where branches had been removed in past times; a black slug was trying to climb it. Dead boughs were scattered about like ichthyosauri in a museum, and beyond them were perishing woodbine stems resembling old ropes.

From the other window all she could see were more trees, in jackets of lichen and stockings of moss. At their roots were stemless yellow fungi like lemons and apricots, and tall fungi with more stem than stool. Next were more trees close together, wrestling for existence, their branches disfigured with wounds, resulting from their mutual rubbings and blows. It was the struggle between these neighbours that she had heard in the night. Beneath them were the rotting stumps of those of the group that had been vanquished long ago, rising from their mossy setting like black teeth from green gums. Further on were other tufts of moss in islands divided by the shed leaves – variety upon variety, dark green and pale green; moss like little fir-trees, like plush, like malachite stars; like nothing on earth except moss.

from *The Woodlanders*
by THOMAS HARDY (1840–1928)

THEY went noiselessly over mats of starry moss, rustled through interspersed tracts of leaves, skirted trunks with spreading roots whose mossed rinds made them like hands wearing green gloves; elbowed old elms and ashes with great forks in which stood pools of water that overflowed on rainy days, and ran down their stems in green cascades. On older trees still than these, huge lumps of fungi grew like lungs. Here, as everywhere, the Unfulfilled Intention, which makes life what it is, was as obvious as it could be among the depraved crowds of a city slum. The lead was deformed, the curve was crippled, the taper was interrupted; the lichen ate the vigour of the stalk, and the ivy slowly strangled to death the promising sapling.

They dived amid beeches under which nothing grew, the younger boughs still retaining their hectic leaves, that rustled in the breeze with a sound almost metallic, like the sheet-iron foliage of the fabled Jarnvid wood.

from *The Woodlanders*
by THOMAS HARDY

OLD favourite tree, thou'st seen time's changes lower,
Though change till now did never injure thee;
For time beheld thee as her sacred dower
And nature claimed thee her domestic tree.
Storms came and shook thee many a weary hour,
Yet stedfast to thy home thy roots have been;
Summers of thirst parched round thy homely bower
Till earth grew iron – still thy leaves were green.
The children sought thee in thy summer shade
And made their playground rings of stick and stone;
The mavis sang and felt himself alone
While in thy leaves his early nest was made,
And I did feel his happiness mine own,
Nought heeding that our friendship was betrayed,
Friend not inanimate – though stocks and stones
There are, and many formed of flesh and bones.

from *The Fallen Elm*
by JOHN CLARE (1793–1864)

The Bird Cherry-Tree

A BIRD cherry had taken root on the path through the hazel-nut grove, and was beginning to choke off the hazel bushes.

For some time I queried whether to cut it down or not to cut it; I felt sorry to do so. This bird cherry did not grow in a clump, but as a tree more than five inches in diameter, and twenty-eight feet high, full of branches, bushy, and wholly covered with bright white, fragrant blossoms. The perfume from it was wafted a long distance.

I certainly should not have cut it down, but one of the workmen – I had given him orders to cut down every bird cherry – began to fell it in my absence. When I came, he had already cut half-way into it, and the sap was dripping down under the axe as he let it fall into the gash.

"There's no help for it," I said to myself; "evidently it is its fate."

So I myself took the axe, and began to help the peasant cut it down.

It is delightful to work at all sorts of work; it is delightful even to cut wood. It is delightful to sink the axe deep in the wood, with a slanting stroke, and then to cut in it straight, and thus to advance deeper and deeper into the tree.

I entirely forget about the bird cherry-tree, and thought only about getting it cut down as quickly as possible.

When I got out of breath, I laid down the axe, and the peasant and I leaned against the tree, and tried to push it over. We pushed hard; the tree shook its foliage and sprinkled us with drops of dew, and strewed all around the white, fragrant petals of its blossoms.

At this instant something shrieked; there was a sharp crackling sound in the centre of the tree, and the tree began to fall.

It broke off near the gash, and slowly wavering, toppled over on the grass, with all its leaves and blossoms. The branches and blossoms trembled for a moment after it fell, and then grew motionless.

"Ekh! what a splendid piece!" said the peasant; "it's a real shame!"

As for me I felt so sorry that I hastened off to the other workmen.

from *The Long Exile and Other Stories for Children*
by LEO TOLSTOI (1828–1910)

CERTAINLY Adam in Paradise had not more sweet and Curious
Apprehensions of the World, than I when I was a child. . . .

    The Corn was Orient* and Immortal Wheat, which never
should be reaped, nor was ever sown: I thought it had stood
from Everlasting to Everlasting. The Dust and Stones of the
Street were as Precious as Gold. The Gates were at first the End
of the World. The Green Trees when I saw them first through
one of the Gates Transported and Ravished me; their Sweetness
and unusual Beauty made my Heart to leap, and almost mad
with Extasie, they were such strange and Wonderfull Things.

*radiant like the dawn

from *The Centuries — Meditations*
by THOMAS TRAHERNE (1637–1674)

The Music of a Tree

ONCE, walking home, I passed beneath a Tree,
   It filled the air like dark stone statuary,
      It was so quiet and still,
      Its thick green leaves a hill
Of strange and faint earth-branching melody:

Over a wall it hung its leaf-starred wood,
And as I lonely there beneath it stood,
      In that sky-hollow street
      Where rang no human feet,
Sweet music flowed and filled me with its flood;

And all my weariness then fell away,
The houses were more lovely than by day;
      The moon and that old Tree
      Sang there, and secretly,
With throbbing heart, tiptoe I stole away.

W. J. TURNER (1889–1946)

BELOW the Hall what meets my eyes?
Ten pine-trees growing near to the steps.
Irregularly scattered, not in ordered line;
In height also strangely unassorted.
The highest of them is thirty feet tall;
The lower scarcely measures ten feet.
They have the air of things growing wild;
Who first planted them no one now knows.
They touch the walls of my blue-tiled house;
Their roots are sunk in the terrace of white sand.
Morning and evening they are visited by the wind and moon;
Rain or fine – they are free from dust and mud.
In the gales of autumn they whisper a vague tune;
From the suns of summer they yield a cool shade.
At the height of spring the fine evening rain
Fills their leaves with a load of hanging pearls.
At the year's end the time of great snow
Stamps their branches with a fret of glittering jade.
At each season they have their varying mood;
Vying in this with any tree that grows.
Last year, when they heard I had bought this house,
Neighbours mocked and the World called me mad –
That a whole family of twice ten souls
Should move house for the sake of a few pines!
Now that I have come to them, what have they given me?
They have only loosened the shackles that bind my heart.
But even so, they are 'profitable friends'
And fill my need of converse with wise men!
Yet when I consider how, still a man of the world,
In belt and cap I scurry through dirt and dust,
From time to time my heart twinges with shame
That I am not fit to be master of my pines!

by PO CHU-I (A.D.821)
from *Chinese Poems* trans. by Arthur Waley

THE talkative Poplar began to chatter like a magpie:

'Little Men! We shall be able to talk to them! We have done with silence! . . . Where do they come from? . . . Who are they?'

And so he rattled on.

The Lime-tree, who was a jolly, fat fellow, came up calmly, smoking his pipe; the conceited and dandified Chestnut-tree screwed his glass into his eye to stare at the Children. He wore a coat of green silk embroidered with pink and white flowers. He thought the little ones too poor-looking and turned away with derision.

'He thinks he's everybody since he has taken to living in town! He despises us!' sneered the Poplar, who was jealous of him.

'Oh dear, oh dear!' wept the Willow, a wretched little stunted fellow, who came clattering along in a pair of wooden shoes too big for him. 'They have come to cut off my head and arms for firewood!'

Tyltyl could not believe his eyes. He never stopped asking the Cat questions:

'Who's this? . . . Who's that? . . .'

And Tylette introduced the soul of each Tree to him.

There was the Elm, who was a sort of shortwinded, paunchy, crabby gnome; the Beech, an elegant, sprightly person; the Birch, who looked like the ghosts in the Palace of Night, with his white flowing garments and his restless gestures. The tallest figure was the Fir-tree: Tyltyl found it very difficult to see his face perched right at the top of his long, thin body; but he looked gentle and sad, whereas the Cypress, who stood near him, dressed all in black, frightened Tyltyl terribly.

However, so far nothing very dreadful had happened. The Trees, delighted at being able to talk, were all chattering together; and our young friend was simply going to ask them where the Blue Bird was hidden, when, all of a sudden, silence reigned. The Trees bowed respectfully and stood aside to make way for an immensely old Oak, dressed in a long gown embroidered with moss and lichen. He leant with one hand on a stick and with the other on a young Oak Sapling who acted as his guide, for the old Oak was blind. His long white beard streamed in the wind.

'It's the King!' said Tyltyl to himself, when he saw his mistletoe crown. 'I will ask him the secret of the forest.'

from *The Children's Blue Bird*
by GEORGETTE LEBLANC MAETERLINCK
after the play *The Blue Bird* by Maeterlinck (1862–1949)

PUCK looked down the meadow that lay all quiet and cool in the shadow of Pook's Hill. A corncrake jarred in a hay-field near by, and the small trouts of the brook began to jump. A big white moth flew unsteadily from the alders, and flapped round the children's heads, and the least little haze of water-mist rose from the brook.

'Do you really want to know?' Puck said.

'We do,' cried the children. 'Awfully!'

'Very good. I promised you that you shall see What you shall see, and you shall hear What you shall hear, though It shall have happened three thousand year; but just now it seems to me that, unless you go back to the house, people will be looking for you. I'll walk with you as far as the gate.'

'Will you be here when we come again?' they asked.

'Surely, sure-ly,' said Puck. 'I've been here some time already. One minute first, please.'

He gave them each three leaves – one of Oak, one of Ash, and one of Thorn.

'Bite these,' said he. 'Otherwise you might be talking at home of what you've seen and heard, and – if I know human beings – they'd send for the doctor. Bite!'

They bit hard, and found themselves walking side by side to the lower gate. Their father was leaning over it.

'And how did your play go?' he asked.

'Oh, splendidly,' said Dan. 'Only afterwards, I think, we went to sleep. It was very hot and quiet. Don't you remember, Una?'

Una shook her head and said nothing.

'I see,' said her father. . . .

. . . 'But why are you chewing leaves at your time of life daughter? For fun?'

'No. It was for something, but I can't exactly remember,' said Una.

And neither of them could till –

from *Puck of Pook's Hill*
by RUDYARD KIPLING (1865–1936)

The Wood Maze

In the forest day by day
I and Bird-in-hand would play.
Hide-and-seek, or touch-and-go
Kept us running to and fro.
Happy on forbidden ground:
Lovely dangers lurked around.

Thus one day her game began:
" Catch me! Catch me, if you can!
  Catch me, catch me!" To her side
Running quickly, oh, I tried! –
Saw her dancing up and down,
Bobbing curls and eyes of brown.

Light of heart, and light of foot,
Sprang she from the hazel-root,
Climbing through the hazel-boughs
Up into the fairies' house:
There a moment cried her fill, –
"Catch me! Catch me!" Then was still.

And the fairies, green and gold,
Lighted down and took soft hold
Of my dear; and like a leaf
Up in air – oh! fairy thief,
Fairy thief! – away sprang she,
Never to come back to me.

In the forest now all day,
Watching how the branches sway,
All alone with mother-wit
Here beneath the boughs I sit
And look up; and, when the breeze
Stirs the leaves upon the trees,
Know that she is one of these.

"Catch me! Catch me!" day by day
That is what they seem to say –
Fairy leaves of green and gold.
Light comes down and takes soft hold, –
Withers them; and then comes wind, –
Shakes them: how the woods are thinned!

Underneath the hazel shade
Here a bed of leaves I've made.
Comfort, comfort, oh! come down,
Bobbing curls and eyes of brown!
Let us end as we began:
Catch me! Catch me, if you can!

Leaf, I cannot tell apart,
Grief for thee hath stretched my heart.
Every leaf that I see fall
Now I love; I keep them all.
Little comforts – such a crumb! –
"Catch me! Catch me!" – down they come.

Long it takes to make the bed
Where together we lie wed.
All alone with mother-wit
Here beneath the boughs I sit:
Down they come! and when the breeze
Lifts the last leaf from the trees,
I shall have her – one of these!

LAURENCE HOUSMAN (1865–1959)

203

What Do the Trees Say

WHAT do the trees say, now it is day?
    "Hush! Hush!
Under our branches the little ones play,
    Hush! Hush!
Creep through the wood, there are elves, there are fays,
Lots of enchantment beyond the sun's rays,
Follow the path where the brown bunny strays,
    Hush! Hush!"

What do the trees say, now it is night?
    "Hush! Hush!
All the big world has been put without light;
    Hush! Hush!
Some little stars in the sky may be peeping,
Just to be sure that all children are sleeping,
While like tall sentinels watch we are keeping,
    Hush! Hush!"

What do the trees say, now we are young?
    "Hush! Hush!
Up in our branches such carols are sung,
    Hush! Hush!
Steal through the shades of this forest of green,
Someone is hiding, but what we have seen
Is seal'd in our silence with things that have been,
    Hush! Hush!"

ANNE MacDONALD (pub. 1923)

In Burnham Beeches

WALKING among these smooth beech-boles
   With cracks and galls
And beetle-holes
   And ivy trickling in green waterfalls,

I noted carvings on their barks,
   Faint and diffuse
As china-marks
   On Worcester or Old Bow: I wondered whose.

I feared that time had played its part
   With those whose token
Was a twin heart,
   So many hearts the swelling bark had broken.

ANDREW YOUNG (1885–1971)

O ROSALIND! these trees shall be my books,
    And in their barks my thought I'll character;
That every eye which in the forest looks
    Shall see thy virtue witness'd every where.
Run, run, Orlando; carve on every tree
The fair, the chaste and unexpressive she.

from As You Like It
by WILLIAM SHAKESPEARE (1563–1616)

SUNK ever in memories, knowing no longer the way,
I came from a green lane from the highroad astray,
And there a scrolled and rusty gateway stood
Holding aloof a bubble: an apple-tree bell,
Which wondering I rang, for down the wood
Went a track long years deserted.
Then sedate as the sound of a knell
It boomed where the trees entwined,
And suddenly large-eyed, leapt from the bracken a hind.
And foxgloves tall in the shade
Stood in procession arrested
Far down in the glade.
There from hazel to hazel the honeysuckle swung
Putting the tangle criss-cross forward and back,
Putting their strands at places over the track,
And boulders and cliffs in the depth of the wood arose,
Haphazard the dells, hot patches, and angles cold,
The high open levels heady and wild,
Banked in with the smell of the small white rose.
I stared through the gate, knowing well,
Well, and of old.
This green, this deserted domain:
I had gone up the road when a child
I must go up the road again.

Here were the woods in childhood I had known;
Here rippled the same flowers on forest paths,
The lyrical light identical; early suns, early moon:
The light that is blown like coloured balloons
In through the curtains at dawn.
That light, earlier than memories,
Early as the day we were born,
Forgotten, remembered till the day we die,
Fluttered through layered slats of those wide trees.
Danced the light there, as goldfinch will fly
In June grasses his flickering way;
Pirouetted the sunlight when the leaves made merry
Leaves that bubble like love-birds
In the blond air.
Lovely the light there,
Lovely the wood in her disarray;
Trees lay in each other's arms, caught so, in the falling.
Had even the movement of men
Destroyed that entangled stillness?
Over these boughs the centuries might pass
In storm, and they remain
Like Chinese trees of jewels within a glass.

from *Lost Forest*
by DOROTHY WELLESLEY (1889–1956)

IT throws a light on her status that our word 'hedge' was derived from the same word as 'hag', a witch. 'Now used' (hag), says *Webster's Dictionary,* 'for an ugly old woman.' The explanation is that hedges were nearly always made of *hawthorn,* peculiarly the property of witches. 'Besom', the familiar garden broom made of twigs (the orthodox witches' horse), is still used, especially in East Anglia, to denote a nasty disagreeable old woman; as is also 'faggot', the bunch of twigs which constitutes the brush. Incidentally, the correct specifications for the occult broomstick were an *ash* handle, to protect the witch from drowning, *birch* twigs for the brush, because when evil spirits were banished some of those in the birch-tree got entangled in the branches and are still there, and *osier* (willow) to bind it in honour of Hecate, the prototype witch to whom it was dedicated, and who, in addition to other plants, also owned belladonna, aconite, mandrake, cyclamen and mint.

from *A Witch's Guide to Gardening*
by DOROTHY JACOB (pub. 1964)
(see p. 217 for evil spirits)

The Fairy Thorn

An Ulster Ballad

"GET up, our Anna dear, from the weary spinning-wheel;
    For your father's on the hill, and your mother is asleep;
Come up above the crags, and we'll dance a highland-reel
    Around the fairy thorn on the steep."

At Anna Grace's door 'twas thus the maidens cried,
    Three merry maidens fair in kirtles of the green;
And Anna laid the rock and the weary wheel aside,
    The fairest of the four, I ween.

They're glancing through the glimmer of the quiet eve,
    Away in milky wavings of neck and ankle bare;
The heavy-sliding stream in its sleepy song they leave,
    And the crags in the ghostly air:

And linking hand in hand, and singing as they go,
    The maids along the hill-side have ta'en their fearless way,
Till they come to where the rowan trees in lonely beauty grow
    Beside the Fairy Hawthorn grey.

The Hawthorn stands between the ashes tall and slim,
    Like matron with her twin grand-daughters at her knee;
The rowan berries cluster o'er low head grey and dim
    In ruddy kisses sweet to see.

The merry maidens four have ranged them in a row,
    Between each lovely couple a stately rowan stem,
And away in mazes wavy, like skimming birds they go,
    Oh, never caroll'd bird like them!

But solemn is the silence of the silvery haze
    That drinks away their voices in echoless repose,
And dreamily the evening has still'd the haunted braes,
    And dreamier the gloaming grows.

And sinking one by one, like lark-notes from the sky
    When the falcon's shadow saileth across the open shaw,
Are hush'd the maiden's voices, as cowering down they lie
    In the flutter of their sudden awe.

For, from the air above, and the grassy ground beneath,
    And from the mountain-ashes and the old Whitethorn
        between,
A Power of faint enchantment doth through their beings
        breathe,
    And they sink down together on the green.

They sink together silent, and stealing side by side,
    They fling their lovely arms o'er their drooping necks so
fair,
Then vainly strive again their naked arms to hide,
    For their shrinking necks again are bare.

Thus clasp'd and prostrate all, with their heads together
bow'd,
    Soft o'er their bosom's beating – the only human sound –
They hear the silky footsteps of the silent fairy crowd,
    Like a river in the air, gliding round.

No scream can any raise, no prayer can any say,
    But wild, wild, the terror of the speechless three –
For they feel fair Anna Grace drawn silently away,
    By whom they dare not look to see.

They feel their tresses twine with her parting locks of gold,
    And the curls elastic falling as her head withdraws;
They feel her sliding arms from their tranced arms unfold,
    But they may not look to see the cause:

For heavy on their senses the faint enchantment lies
    Through all that night of anguish and perilous amaze;
And neither fear nor wonder can ope their quivering eyes,
    Or their limbs from the cold ground raise,

Till out of night the earth has roll'd her dewy side,
    With every haunted mountain and streamy vale below;
When, as the mist dissolves in the yellow morning tide,
    The maidens' trance dissolveth so.

Then fly the ghastly three as swiftly as they may,
    And tell their tale of sorrow to anxious friends in vain –
They pined away and died within the year and day,
    And ne'er was Anna Grace seen again.

SIR SAMUEL FERGUSON (1810–1886)

'I HAVE been sketching other things which are full of old times.' These 'other things' were the quartet and quintet on which work progressed in the intervals of woodcutting and bonfires. Alice's diary is especially valuable in regard to the quintet: 'Wonderful weird beginning – same atmosphere as "Owls" – evidently reminiscence of sinister trees & impression of Flexham Park . . .' 'Sad "dispossessed" trees & their dance & unstilled regret for their evil fate – or rather curse – wh. brought it on . . .' 'The sinister trees & their strange dance in it – then a wail for their sin – wonderful.' Flexham Park was near Fittleworth. A group of withered trees there was connected by the inhabitants with a fraternity of Spanish monks who had once lived there. While participating in some form of black magic they were, according to local legend, struck by lightning and turned into trees. This was the sort of lore that excited Elgar, who was in any case fascinated by trees, as we know from *Caractacus* and his exultant phrase to Jaegar, 'The trees are singing my music – or have I sung theirs?'

from *Portrait of Elgar*
by MICHAEL KENNEDY (pub. 1968)

Trees in the Moonlight

TREES in the moonlight stand
  Still as a steeple,
And so quiet they seem like ghosts
  Of country people –

Dead farmers and their wives
  Of long, long ago,
Haunting the countryside
  They used to know;

Old gossips and talkers
  With tongues gone still;
Ploughmen rooted in the land
  They used to till;

Old carters and harvesters,
  Their wheels long rotten;
Old maids whose very names
  Time has forgotten.

Ghosts are they hereabouts;
  Them the moon sees,
Dark and still in the fields
  Like sleeping trees.

Long nights in autumn
  Hear them strain and cry,
Torn with a wordless sorrow
  As the gale sweeps by.

Spring makes fresh buds appear
  On the old boughs,
As if it could to their old wishes
  These ghosts arouse.

Trees in the summer night
  By moonlight linger on
So quiet they seem like ghosts
  Of people gone,

And it would be small wonder
  If at break of day
They heard the far-off cock-crow
  And fled away.

JAMES REEVES (1909–1978)

213

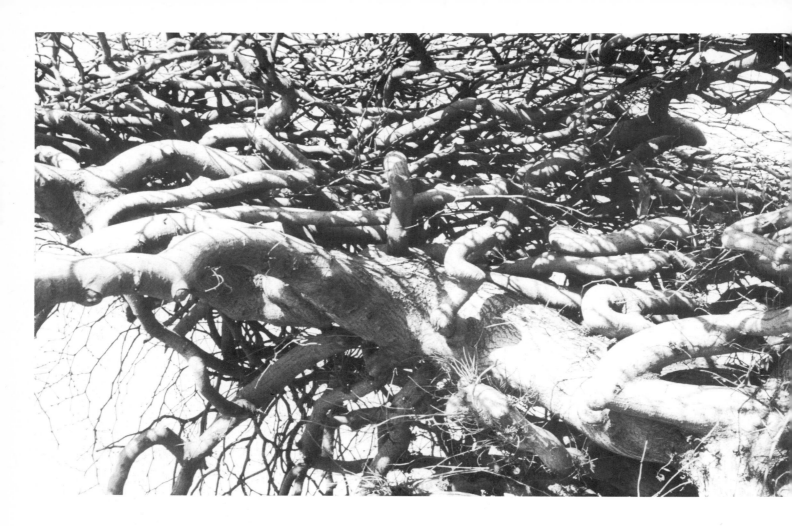

THEN Thor blushed with shame at his own weakness, which had made him regret his strength; and, without any more grumbling or hanging back, he plunged into the dreadful river-clouds, whose dark vapours closed around him and covered him. He was hidden from sight, and the Æsir went on their way over the glittering bridge.

Daintily and airily they trod over it; they swung themselves up the swinging arch; they reached its summit on a pale, bright cloud. Thor was there already waiting for them, drenched and weary, but cheerful and bold. Then, all together, they knocked at the door of the pale, bright cloud; it blew open, and they passed in. Oh! then what did they see! Looking up to an infinite height through the purple air, they saw towering above them Yggdrasil's fairest branches, leafy and of a tender green, which also stretched far and wide; but, though they looked long, the Æsir could distinguish no topmost bough, and it almost seemed to them that, from somewhere up above, this mighty earth-tree must draw another root, so firmly and so tall it grew. On one side stood the Palace of the Norns, which was so bright that it almost blinded them to look at, and on the other the Urda fountain plashed its cool waters – rising, falling, glittering, as nothing ever glitters on this side the clouds.

Heroes of Asgard
by A. and E. KEARY

The Two Trees

BELOVED, gaze in thine own heart,
The holy tree is growing there;
From joy the holy branches start,
And all the trembling flowers they bear.
The changing colours of its fruit
Have dowered the stars with merry light;
The surety of its hidden root
Has planted quiet in the night
The shaking of its leafy head
Has given the waves their melody,
And made my lips and music wed,
Murmuring a wizard song for thee.
There the Loves a circle go,
The flaming circle of our days,
Gyring, spiring to and fro
In those great ignorant leafy ways;
Remembering all that shaken hair
And how the wingèd sandals dart,
Thine eyes grow full of tender care:
Beloved, gaze in thine own heart.

Gaze no more in the bitter glass
The demons, with their subtle guile,
Lift up before us when they pass,
Or only gaze a little while;
For there a fatal image grows
That the stormy night receives,
Roots half hidden under snows,
Broken bows and blackened leaves.
For all things turn to barrenness
In the dim glass the demons hold,
The glass of outer weariness,
Made when God slept in times of old.
There, through the broken branches, go
The ravens of unresting thought;
Flying, crying, to and fro,
Cruel claw and hungry throat,
Or else they stand and sniff the wind,
And shake their ragged wings; alas!
Thy tender eyes grow all unkind:
Gaze no more in the bitter glass.

W. B. YEATS (1865–1939)

LET the only consistency
In the course of my poetry
Be like that of the hawthorn tree
Which in early Spring breaks
Fresh emerald, then by nature's law
Darkens and deepens and takes
Tints of purple-maroon, rose-madder and straw.

Sometimes these hues are found
Together, in pleasing harmony bound.
Sometimes they succeed each other. But through
All the changes in which the hawthorn is dight,
No matter in what order, one thing is sure
- The haws shine ever the more ruddily bright!

And when the leaves have passed
Or only in a few tatters remain
The tree to the winter condemned
         Stands forth at last
      Not bare and drab and pitiful,
But a candelabrum of oxidised silver gemmed
By innumerable points of ruby
Which dominate the whole and are visible
Even at considerable distance
As flame-points of living fire.
That so it may be
With my poems too at last glance
Is my only desire.

All else must be sacrificed to this great cause.
I fear no hardships. I have counted the cost.
I with my heart's blood as the hawthorn with its haws
Which are sweetened and polished by the frost!

See how these haws burn, there down the drive,
In this autumn air that feels like cotton wool,
When the earth has the gelatinous limpness of a body
      dead as a whole
While its tissues are still alive!

Poetry is human existence come to life,
The glorious energy that once employed
Turns all else in creation null and void,
The flower and fruit, the meaning and goal,
Which won all else is needs removed by the knife
Even as a man who rises high
Kicks away the ladder he has come up by.

from *In the Fall*
by HUGH MacDIARMID (1892–1978)

THE scenes are desert now, and bare,
Where flourish'd once a forest fair,
When these waste glens with copse were lined,
And peopled with the hart and hind.
Yon Thorn – perchance whose prickly spears
Have fenced him for three hundred years,
While fell around his green compeers –
Yon lonely Thorn, would he could tell
The changes of his parent dell,
Since he, so gray and stubborn now,
Waved in each breeze a sapling bough;

Would he could tell how deep the shade
A thousand mingled branches made;
How broad the shadows of the oak,
How clung the rowan to the rock,
And through the foliage show'd his head,
With narrow leaves and berries red;
What pines on every mountain sprung,
O'er every dell what birches hung,
In every breeze what aspens shook,
What alders shaded every brook!

from *Marmion*
by SIR WALTER SCOTT (1771–1832)
(referring to Ettrick Forest)

The Hill Pines Were Sighing

THE hill pines were sighing,
O'ercast and chill was the day:
A mist in the valley lying
Blotted the pleasant May.

But deep in the glen's bosom
Summer slept in the fire
Of the odorous gorse-blossom
And the hot scent of the brier.

A ribald cuckoo clamoured,
And out of the copse the stroke
Of the iron axe that hammered
The iron heart of the oak.

Anon a sound appalling,
As a hundred years of pride
Crashed, in the silence falling:
And the shadowy pine-trees sighed.

ROBERT BRIDGES (1844–1930)

Cherry-Tree Poems (I)

I amputate your limbs,
but in whose arm lies the disease?

You're stealing light you know.
My flowers, my grass, have died
on your account.
Your flowers last
two weeks at most.
Restoring balance,
that's my job;
your roots will compensate,
you will not fall.
I've waited till the autumn,
watched your wounds,
taken too little, not too much,
and you must understand
I'm nature too,
monstrous, but natural
unlike you,
whom I have taught conformity.
You should be grateful, for without
this slight curtailment
I'd have been
your executioner.

But when I put the residue
of your offence upon the fire,
you hiss at me.

JOHN PURSER (1942–

. . . THAT such woods as do yet remain entire might be carefully preserved, and such as are destroyed, sedulously repaired: it is what all persons who are owners of land may contribute to, and with infinite delights, as well as profit, who are touched with that laudable ambition of imitating their illustrious ancestors, and of worthy serving their generation. To these my earnest and humble advice should be, that at their very first coming to their estates, and as soon as they get children, they would seriously think of this work of propagation also: for I observe that there is no part of husbandry which men commonly more fail in, neglect, and have cause to repent of, than that they did not begin planting betimes, without which they can expect neither fruit, ornament or delight from their labours. Men seldom plant trees till they begin to be wise, that is, till they grow old, and find, by experience, the prudence and necessity of it. When Ulysees, after a ten year absence, was returned from Troy, and coming home, found his aged father in the field planting trees, he asked him, "Why, being so advanced in years, he would put himself to the fatigue and labour of planting that, of which he was never likely to enjoy the fruits?". The good old man, taking him for a stranger, gently replied: "I plant" says he "against when my son Ulysees comes home."

from *Sylva* or *A Discourse of Forest Trees*
by JOHN EVELYN (1620–1706)

Tree-Planting

PLANT here, for other eyes, that kingly tree
    Whose reign we shall not see.
Choose well the spot, that other eyes may bless
    Its natural loveliness.
Let them not guess what loving pains we took,
    Or how we paused to look
From every knoll, and every vantage ground
    In all the landscape round,
That one invisible tree one day shall fill
    Its place upon the hill,
Give to our vanished thought its perfect form,
    And stand against the storm,
Playing its own true parts, when we are gone,
    For you my little son.

ALFRED NOYES (1880–1959)

'Trees' in No. 10 Protest

SIX human trees waddled up to 10 Downing Street yesterday
to urge the Government to do more to safeguard the ozone
layer and protect the rain forests. Campaigners from the
United Nations Association Youth Council dressed as trees to
make their point and handed in 22 horse chestnut saplings at
No. 10 – one for each member of the Cabinet.

from *The Yorkshire Post*
13 March 1989

A Tree in the City

AT last on the little black tree
in the city square,
There is a green leaf.

Hesitating,
A ray of the sun, comes down.
It is a white finger of light,
Pointing to life.

In the offices,
The row of pale faces are lifted,
They are turned to the green spark,
Unlit candles, wistful for flame.

They are not dreaming,
Merely of the distant countryside,
Of passing loveliness.
They know, that loveliness
Runs out, even through privileged hearts,
Like sand through an hour glass.
They want to begin to live,
And to live for ever.

The spark of life
In each of their souls
Is a gem in a locked casket.
It suddenly burns more brightly.
Waxes and wanes,
Like a breathing ember.

Now it could be fanned to a great flame,
by a mere breath.
Will no one come,
Into the city of London,
With the gift in his breath,
To answer,
The people's wordless supplication
For Life?

CARYLL HOUSELANDER (1901–1954)

226

Child's Song in Spring

THE silver birch is a dainty lady,
    She wears a satin gown;
The elm tree makes the old churchyard shady,
    She will not live in town.

The English oak is a sturdy fellow,
    He gets his green coat late;
The willow is smart in a suit of yellow.
    While brown the beech-trees wait.

Such a gay green gown God gives the larches—
    As green as He is good!
The hazels hold up their arms for arches
    When Spring rides through the wood.

The chestnut's proud, and the lilac's pretty,
    The poplar's gentle and tall,
But the plane tree's kind to the poor dull city –
    I love him best of all.

E. NESBIT (1858–1924)

THE blue sky, the brown soil beneath, the grass, the trees, the animals, the wind, the rain, and stars are never strange to me; for I am in, and of, and am one with, them; and my flesh and the soil are one and the heat in my blood and in the sunshine are one, and the winds and the tempests and my passions are one. I feel the "strangeness" only with regard to my fellow-men, especially in towns, where they exist in conditions unnatural to me, but congenial to them.

from *Hampshire Days*
by W. H. HUDSON (1841–1922)

THE budding twigs spread out their fan
    To catch the breezy air;
And I must think, do all I can,
    That there is pleasure there.

If this belief from heaven be sent,
    If such be Nature's plan,
Have I not reason to lament
    What man has made of man?

from *Lines Written in Early Spring*
by WILLIAM WORDSWORTH (1770–1850)

YET it was in Huby, a village I never learned to love that I had the nearest thing I had encountered to a mystical experience at Riffa Wood. A paved footpath went through that wood. The stones had once been a Roman chariot way. In Spring, in bluebell time, I went that way.

The wood was very still. An oak spread its branches across the path. I sensed something deep and primitive in it, drawing me to it as to something holy. I draped the trunk with my arms. My feet stirred the leaf-mould of many a summer. I felt as though my feet were joining the roots of the tree. Digging deep, deep, drawing sap from the earth. Drawing the life-sap up, up into the tree that was one with my body. Up to the branches, to the twigs, the leaves, sap rising to the tree's flowering, which in springtime must happen before the fruit is formed and the seed which renews the life of the tree.

I pressed my fingertips into the crannies of the bark. In a kind of oneness I felt the sap rise, the pulsing of my own blood through my fingertips. I knew the moment of ecstacy, the standing apart from the body and the body of the tree seemed to be one and not one. Between one heartbeat and the next I had known mystic experience, which has its being outside time and in eternity. And in that timeless communion was at one with that universal nature in which we both had our roots.

So in my two golden years, I passed through the wood of dreams and in passing, brushed, who knows, against ultimate reality. In the nearest thing on earth to the garden of Eden, that is to say, childhood, I had become aware of the tree of knowledge of good and evil. In Riffa Wood, I believe I touched the tree God forbade Adam to touch – the tree of Life.

from *The Edge of Darkness, Edge of Light*
by R. C. SCRIVEN (blind author)

Go towards the high growing Trees.
And before one of them
Which is beautiful high growing and mighty,
Say thou these words:
Hail be unto Thee!
Oh good living Tree,
Made by the Creator.

In the days of old when Creation was young,
The earth was filled with giant trees,
Whose branches soared above the clouds,
And in them dwelled our Ancient Fathers,
They who walked with the Angels,
And who lived by the Holy Law.
In the shadow of their branches all men lived in peace,
And wisdom and knowledge was theirs,
And the revelation of the Endless Light.
Through their forests flowed the Eternal River,
And in the centre stood the Tree of Life,
And it was not hidden from them.
They ate from the table of Earthly Mother,
And slept in the arms of the Heavenly Father,
And their covenant was for eternity with the Holy Law.
In that time the trees were the brothers of men,
And their span on earth was very long,
As long as the Eternal River,
Which flowed without ceasing
From the Unknown Spring.
Now the desert sweeps the earth with burning sand,
The giant trees are dust and ashes,
And the wide river is a pool of mud.
For the sacred covenant with the Creator
Was broken by the sons of men.
And they were banished from their home of trees.
Now the path leading to the Tree of Life
Is hidden from the eyes of men,
And sorrow fills the empty sky
Where once the lofty branches soared.
Now into the burning desert
Come the Children of Light,
To labour in the Garden of the Brotherhood.
The seed they plant in the barren soil
Will become a mighty forest
And trees shall multiply
And spread their wings of green
Until the whole earth be covered once again.
The whole earth shall be a garden
And the tall trees shall cover the land.
In that day shall sing the Children of Light a new song:
My brother, Tree!
Let me not hide myself from thee,
But let us share the breath of life
Which our Earthly Mother has given to us.

More beautiful than the first jewel
Of the rug maker's art,
Is the carpet of green leaves under my bare feet;
More majestic than the silken canopy
Of the rich merchant,
Is the tent of branches above my head,
Through which the bright stars give light.
The wind among the leaves of the cypress
Maketh a sound like unto a chorus of angels.
Through the rugged oak and royal cedar
The Earthly Mother hath sent a message of Eternal Life
To the Heavenly Father.
My prayer goeth forth unto the tall trees:
And their branches reaching skyward
Shall carry my voice to the Heavenly Father.
For each child thou shalt plant a tree,
That the womb of thy Earthly Mother
Shall bring forth life,
As the womb of woman doth bring forth life.

from *The Gospel of the Essenes*
(written circa 100 B.C.–A.D.70)
trans. by E. B. Szekely

SUDDENLY I was aware of its skyward-reaching arms and upturned finger-tips, as if some vivid life (or electricity) was streaming through them far into the spaces of heaven, and drawing the same energies from below. The day was quite still and there was no movement in the branches, but in that moment the tree was no longer a separate or separable organism, but a vast being ramifying far into space, sharing and uniting the life of Earth and Sky, and full of a most amazing activity.

The reader of this will probably have had some similar experiences . . . and he will have known that these creatures are but likenesses of himself, intimately and deeply-related to him in their love and hunger longing, and like himself too, unfathomed and unfathomable.

from *Pagan and Christian Creeds*
by EDWARD CARPENTER (1844–1929)

FOR this Tree does afterwards plentifully bring forth Leaves, to shelter and shadow its fruit: as if it should say, according to our Blessed Saviour's expression, *First seek the Kingdom of Heaven*; First bloom in *Virtue*, nourish'd by the sap of *Grace*, spreading itself from the *Root* of Christian Humility, into all the Boughs and Branches; that is, into all your Actions; *and all other things shall be added unto you*. Leaves shall not be wanting, that is, Cloaths to cover you; besides other Necessaries, which are all in fine but Leaves: Nay, Honours and Dignities, what are they but withering Leaves? What, Wealth or rich Apparel, but Leaves, whereof Man is soon despoil'd, and left poor and naked? What, voluptuous Pleasures, but Leaves, which so soon as enjoy'd shrink up and vanish?

Oh! what a bleak Autumn and Fall of Leaf (sudden, and unexpected) is that we find in this our vale of Misery? Who then would not be *poor* in *Spirit*, and *naked* in his *Affections* to the leafy Creatures of this transitory Life, that he may bloom to Eternity?

from an English Emblem Book *Ashrea*
by E. M. 1665
(exact authorship uncertain)

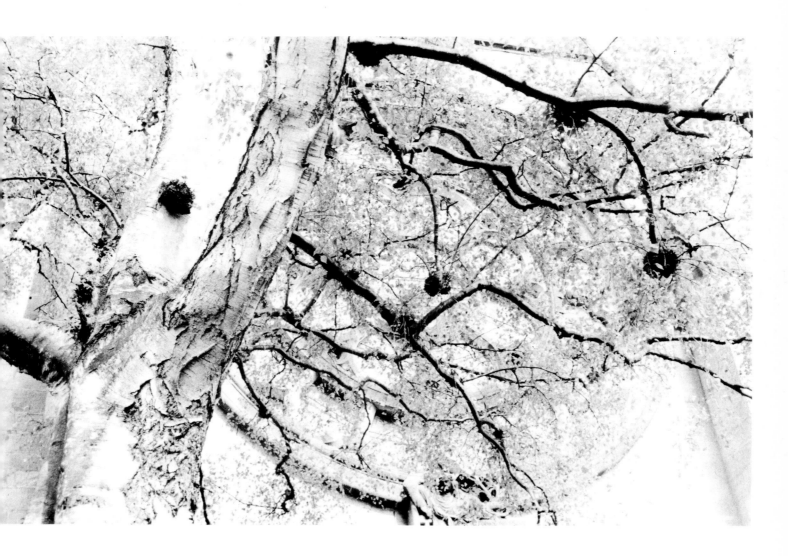

O TREE of many branches! One thou hast
Thou barest not, but grafted'st on thee. Now,
Should all men's thunders break on thee, and leave
Thee reft of bough and blossom, that one branch
Shall cling to thee, my Father, Brother, Friend,
Shall cling to thee, until the end of end.

FRANCIS THOMPSON (1859–1907)

THERE grew a goodly tree him faire beside,
    Loaden with fruit and apples rosie red,
    As they in pure vermilion had beene dide,
    Whereof great vertues over all were red:
    For happie life to all, which thereon fed,
    And life eke everlasting did befall:
    Great God it planted in that blessed sted
    With his almightie hand, and did it call
The tree of life, the crime of our first father's fall.

In all the world like was not to be found,
    Save in that soile, where all good things did grow,
    And freely sprong out of the fruitfull ground,
    As incorrupted Nature did them sow,
    Till that dread Dragon all did overthrow.
    Another like faire tree eke grew thereby,
    Whereof who so did eat, eftsoones did know
    Both good and ill: O mornefull memory:
That tree through one man's fault hath doen us all to dy.

From that first tree forth flowd, as from a well,
    A trickling streame of Balme, most soveraine
    And daintie deare, which on the ground still fell,
    And overflowèd all the fertill plaine,
    And it had deawèd bene with timely raine:
    Life and long health that gratious ointment gave,
    And deadly woundes could heale, and reare againe
    The senseless corse appointed for the grave.
Into that same he fell: which did from death him save.

red = told
eke = also
eftsoones = immediately after
corse = corpse

from *The Faerie Queene*
by EDMUND SPENSER (1552–1599)

LOOK closer, and you may find the leaves are yellowing and twigs curving. . . . The reason? Opinions differ but the overwhelming weight of evidence points to air pollution as the cause.

In 1985, World Wide Fund for Nature UK gave a grant to Friends of the Earth to carry out a survey of beech and yew trees in England. Over 500 volunteers took part, and more than 3,000 trees were surveyed. The result confirmed the more pessimistic estimates – 69% of beech and 68% of yew showed the damage symptoms commonly known as tree dieback. Although at the time these disturbing figures were dismissed by the Government and the Forestry Commission, last year's Tree Health Survey, carried out by the Forestry Commission, produced figures which were even worse. The Forestry Commission found that a staggering 92% of the 672 beech trees surveyed showed some degree of defoliation. The percentage of the 767 oak trees surveyed was the same.

Extract from an article by TESSA ROBERTSON,
Conservation Officer, in the W.W.F
(World Wide Fund for Nature) *Journal*, summer 1988.

The address of the W.W.F. is Panda House, Wayside Park, Godalming, Surrey.

How many of the woods and trees that you knew from childhood still stand?

In the last 40 years almost half of our ancient woods have vanished. More than 109,000 miles of hedgerows across Britain have been grubbed up – enough to stretch almost five times around the world!

Britain's native broadleaved trees are disappearing faster than they are being replaced. Unless we act now many of our most precious woods will be destroyed or irreparably damaged.

This will mean fewer places for you and your children to enjoy the countryside. Fewer refuges for birds and animals that need shelter and food.

We owe it to future generations to save woodland and to replace lost trees. The need is urgent and it's being answered now by the Woodland Trust.

from a pamphlet issued
by the Woodland Trust

The address of the Woodland Trust is Autumn Park, Dysert Road, Grantham, Lincolnshire.

Author Index

Photographic Index